# Meditation Breakthrough For the Western World

## Bridge to Eternity

Dr. Ralph B. White, M.S.D.

Published by White Light Publishers
Hazelwood, NC

Copyright © 1996 By Ralph B. White
All rights reserved
including the right of reproduction
in whole or in part in any form.

Published by White Light Publishers
P. O. Box 499
Hazelwood, NC 28738-0499

Library of Congress Catalog Card Number 95-91012

**ISBN 0–9651085–0–3**

Manufactured in the United States of America

## DEDICATION

This book is dedication to my beloved wife, without whose assistance it may not have been written.

## ACKNOWLEDGEMENTS

My heartfelt thanks to the many special angels for their untiring assistance in helping me share their unconditional love with all humanity.

Many thanks to the advanced students of this meditation for their faithfulness, dedication and assistance.

With deep appreciation to the many students who study with me, for their wonderful cooperation and permission to use some of their special experiences as examples quoted herein.

# Foreword

Some call it Clairvoyance. It has been with me since childhood, and to me it is perfectly normal. Flashes of insight and knowing the consequences beforehand, dulled the lure of temptations that might have otherwise led me into harms way. I considered it natural, an ability that everyone possessed, and a personal ability, never to be shared with anyone else.

Much later in life I learned that the opposite was true. Most people had learned to fear it, yet almost everyone had the latent ability. Only a few had allowed it to develop, yet it was as near as looking within and seeking to find it.

It is another world. Only a single dimension separates it from ours. You can find it within yourself. You can make that inner contact in quiet moments of introspection It appears in a dreamlike reality, sometimes in pictures, more often as hunches or intuition.

These facts should have been made available to everyone years ago. I had hoped some older and more experiencd person would tell you the real truth. Now, after seventy-seven years of living in and thoroughly enjoying both worlds, I fear there may be no one else. Therefore, I present that world to you today as a *fait accompli,* a fact that has already been accomplished.

There are people anxious to tell startling experiences and convictions. Most of them would be different from my own, and questionable. Mine comes to you in the form of a Meditation Breakthrough, created for us here in the Western World. The great number of students who can duplicate my own experiences attests to the validity and efficacy of this amazing breakthrough.

This might be considered a sequel to my book *Cosmic Fire, a Guide to the Masters' Meditation,* since it continues with the same subject, and along the same time line. Each book, however, is complete and tells a different story about the same subject. The first tells of its discovery and beginning, the second of its subsequent development.

The first three chapters of this book are a continuing account of my learning and teaching events. Then, quite unexpectedly, an event occurred that accelerated the movement of our teaching experiences forward, and then lifted them upward into unimaginable dimensions.

The unusual nature of these remarkable happenings followed a near death encounter about two years ago that might well have taken my life. While there are many near death similarities, it happened quite unlike any of the other such experiences that have previously been reported. As the result, a great amount of unknown information about higher dimensions of existence now flows freely from that source

The amazing character of these happenings is of great importance to everyone's understanding of reality, for it moves beyond much of what has been written on that subject. The reality of my personal contact with the next higher dimension become clearer and more real, and the volume of information flowing to me from that source increased dramatically.

You will note that I will speak more to the near death experience and to the knowledge that flows from it, than to my own personal life, for few people are interested in reading about an existence where life is peaceful, happy, where all needs are met, and filled with spiritual and physical love. Life without its usual conflict generates little interest.

In stark contrast to the above, information continues to flow from out of this amazing death experience. It comes to me in such an exciting manner that the quality of my life became elevated several levels upward in the direction of infinity.

Excitement abounds in every contact it brings. The sheer volume of knowledge filled the remainder of this book with a continuing flow that has already given me enough left over to make a good beginning on another.

My introduction to this subject occurred a long time ago, when my special instruction began on my first ocean voyage to the Orient after World War II. It continued for many years, beginning with a teacher from Tibet. Within a year, two additional guides or teachers from a higher level of consciousness joined in my instruction.

My position as Captain of the ship afforded me spare time to devote to the special study given me at different times by these unique teachers. Under such powerful instructors, I entered into a world of little known information and knowledge. I found it easy to become a good student, and quickly advanced.

The same two special guides or masters still work with me today, devoting all of their time exclusively to monitoring and assisting in the events described herein. Over time, others of equal talent joined the teaching staff. My education continues.

My mission is to emphasize another side of life from what most people seem to prefer. For well over thirty years of the original phase, it dealt with the successful completion of two demanding careers without physical or mental exhaustion. The ability to excel in both developed as benefits from a special study of philosophy and special meditation that I was privileged to pursue concurrent with my occupations.

They had a good reason to select me as messenger to offer their method again to earth's people. According to their calculations, everything was ready and the time had come. I had attained a position of great responsibility at an early age, while still struggling to prove myself.

If I could successfully meet the responsibility of commanding an ocean liner through the thousands of instant decisions necessary to protect lives and property from the perils of the sea, and study and practice meditation at the same time, it would move meditation from the category of an arm chair experience into one of meeting the challenge of the rugged life of a business professional and that of a master mariner.

My successful completion of two such careers proved their assessment to be correct. Along the way, I found the meditation the most powerful asset a person could ever have. Among other things, it saved my life three times that I know of, and in one of those instances, with only a single thought that came into my mind at the right moment, it saved my life, a ship and 103 souls from a watery grave.

Needless to say, that incident alone convinced me this special meditation deserved a place in the life of everyone who aspire to move their lives from out of the mundane into the Eternal Presence which contains easy answers to what we usually think of as problems.

I know it can do the same for the readers of this book.

My two teaching masters continue to lead me nightly into higher levels of meditative contact. Chapter IV shows the extent of their plan to teach me how to make still better use of my time.

They allowed me to unexpectedly endure a near death experience with all of its uncertainties, but with one difference from the other reported incidents. At the end of the ordeal, they gave me a guided tour of eternity.

At that high level, they showed me the length and breadth of Creation, and the everlasting life others who had gone before were already experiencing. Most of all, they taught me how to take some of my most advanced students into a limited access of that level, and show them some of the same scenes they had shown me earlier. As they continue to meditate and develop, some of them are already achieving the ability to go there on their own.

This information should enable you to understand what has happened before well enough to accompany me on the exciting journey that follows. While I filled the position of a scribe, my teachers wrote the exciting scenes that fill this narrative.

It is their book. They took me through the adventures that follow. Using the typing skill they taught me as a court reporter, they guided my hand as it wrote these thoughts that brings their wisdom and guidance to a world in desperate need of a way back to something beautiful it lost long, long ago.

It is to this end that I offer their wisdom to everyone.

## CONTENTS

| Chapter | Title | Page |
|---|---|---|
| 1 | Introduction | 1 |
| 2 | A Troubling Vision | 7 |
| 3 | The Whirlwind | 15 |
| 4 | The Ascension | 23 |
| 5 | The Cosmos | 31 |
| 6 | The Awakening | 43 |
| 7 | Ascension Revisited | 49 |
| 8 | The Cosmic Whirlwind | 59 |
| 9 | New Home | 71 |
| 10 | The Real Truth | 79 |
| 11 | Tschen Li | 87 |
| 12 | An angels view of planet earth | 94 |
| 13 | Free Will and Karma | 103 |
| 14 | Students visit Angelic Realm | 115 |
| 15 | The Masters' Meditation & Reiki | 121 |
| 16 | Mother Mary Appears | 129 |
| 17 | Mother Mary Continues | 139 |
| 18 | Mona | 147 |
| 19 | The Final Results | 155 |
| 20 | Mother Mary Speaks | 163 |
| 21 | The Meditation | 179 |

## Meditation Breakthrough
for the Western World

### Bridge to Eternity

### Chapter I
Introduction

"Are you ready to teach others how to access the secret power of the universe?" The voice of my teacher echoed through my brain in the middle of the night.

"I have only had three hours sleep," I protested to her fading voice, my body shivering from cold. The confusion of the unexpected awakening and the opening of a forbidden subject added additional bewilderment.

"Do you wonder why the existence of this miracle remains hidden in this so-called age of expanding information?" She continued.

"Why do you want to talk about it now?" I asked.

She said. "The masters and angels have just decided that you are to advise your regular students of this new policy, and find an easy way to tell new people of its possibility."

"Send me back to the half-sleep mode," I said, "and tell me the rest in pictures."

"Half-sleep is also half-awake," I thought, knowing that she would pick up the thought even as my body eased itself gently into a deep relaxation. It promised to be a long night.

The combined minds of my two master teachers linked closely to mine from another dimension. Slowly, one by one, vivid scenes containing pictorial representations of the knowledge they wanted to impress into my higher mind flowed past, as if in a dream. The information would still be available for my review the following morning, and a new chapter in the book they wanted me write would be well under way.

Then came the final thought for the night, "You can also access that secret power and make it the part of your life it was meant to be in the beginning."

In an intensifying rapture of deep sleep, I remembered I had been using the method for years. I had touched the fringes of that secret as a three year-old. A special guide made himself known under rather unusual circumstances. When I finally understood he came from the highest level of Creation, I gladly accepted his offer of assistance.

He had promised to help me through childhood's difficulties. With his help, I always knew the proper path to take for the most acceptable results. This enabled me to enjoy a more peaceful yet acceptable pattern of existence. When in need, my guide always came to be with me, especially during the hectic days of World War II. I felt his presence during the uncertain moments of conflict. His spiritual love surrounded me with its protection during periods of danger. No one in my group ever suffered a serious injury, while other groups around us were not so fortunate.

My faith in his guidance reached the point of absolute trust when the cessation of hostilities found me as Captain of an ocean liner while still a very young man. It was all part of their Divine plan. That plan became clear when a new teacher came to be with me during my first voyage to the Far East.

## Chapter I

He appeared in the robe of a monk and I accepted him as that. A little later, I learned he was a Tibetan Lama and a physician, on specific assignment. When he offered to teach me a special philosophy and meditation, I initially refused. When he took me into a beautiful meditation from a distant location, the beauty and magnitude of the experience changed my mind.

He showed me how this method could merge perfectly with the life style of my own Western World. The vision of its easy accessibility and dynamic results excited me with its promise. I saw in an instant how it could enhance the lives of everyone fortunate enough to accept and use it, and make it a part of their personal contact with their inner selves.

I then became his student with a verbal arrangement that endured for over thirty-two years. It ended only with his transition into a higher state of consciousness. The process changed my life forever.

I sailed the sea lanes of the world for the next twenty-one years in the same capacity. My position as Captain gave me the time and privacy to meditate and study in the quiet of my room on my time off.

No one of those around me knew of my studies. The natural result of this meditation automatically led me to excel in my work. I tell of this special result for the benefit of those who wish to study this method through the home study course I teach. It is through this study that the secret power of the universe can be attained.

A welcome change came into my life from the special guidance of my Tibetan teacher who was assisted by other highly advanced instructors I met and studied with in that area. You will be introduced to some of those special masters, as I tell you how they used their own unique abilities to help me, and to help any of my students if they only ask.

In this experience you will be introduced to the Masters' Meditation. You will follow my experiences as the Masters show me the many steps into an enlightened consciousness. Then you will be able to follow me into the spectacular awareness of the angelic world of the ascended masters.

You will go with me and my masters as they take me meditatively into many special locations within their own universe. Share every occurrence with me as each one becomes a learning experience and attunes me to its own special energy. All will be described in detail. This will allow you to share in the many powerful revelations accessible to everyone who uses this method.

It is those procedures, created by masters and angels, that make the dynamism of the Masters' Meditation so powerful. Whenever you meditate with me, or do it alone after you have learned the process, the masters and angels are with you whether or not you are aware of it.

The need for this special awakening contact is now growing stronger. Many people feel the need to go within themselves, seeking answers our institutions somehow fail to give them. *Belonging* to one or more groups no longer fills the need for an intimate personal relationship with Creation. Membership in this, the masters' all-inclusive group of meditators, costs little effort and the rewards are out of this world.

The meditation is a rewarding experience. It fills you with peace and joy as you contact advanced levels of the higher consciousness at your own pace. You develop

## Chapter I

these skills rapidly, all from the level of your awareness from which you entered the program. Each of your five physical senses, are one by one or collectively opened at your higher level of consciousness.

Many begin the meditation with some or all of these senses already open. It is never in one's interest to compare his or her progress with that of someone else. We are all where we should be, and are the by-product of lifetimes of experiences.

This special meditation is the masters' and angels' gift to humanity, It is their method to bring as many of us as possible back to the path leading to Creation. We have our choice, and the alternative is not pleasant. Anyone who cares to look should remember the words of one of our greatest teachers, "He who has eyes, let him see."

You be the judge. If you are concerned about the chaos you see everywhere about us, this meditation is the best alternative I have found in many years of searching. The growing number of people following this special path attest to the satisfaction they have found in its high level of celestial contact, and in the balance it has brought to their earthly existence.

If, after you experience it, you feel as I and thousands of other students do, that it can make an important contribution to the survival of our world and its inhabitants, please add your voice to ours. Join with us, and with the masters and angels that created and still monitor this very important method. Tell others about this way to beat the unfavorable odds that face us. We *can* change those odds in our favor.

In this book we begin where my last book, *Cosmic Fire*, ended. We continue here where I left off my long years of study in order to learn how to teach this meditation and its attendant philosophy to the world, and began to teach it to everyone who would listen.

The masters and angels have assisted all the way. It is their method and reflects their desire to help us, if we but ask. They will continue to assist me as I teach and to work on an individual basis with everyone who has found this path and are now following it.

These teachers have led the main focus of this present work into the development and presentation of additional meditations. These now enable me to present a wider range of meditations to the advancing student. Each meditation is capable of standing alone in its intensity and benefits, and leading the student into amazingly powerful experiences and development.

And it is within one of these powerful meditative experiences the student accesses the secret power of the universe. Within it we find unlimited areas for development, growth, and attainment.

My teachers have assisted me in recording these meditations on cassette tapes and combining them in a progressive order. We now have an inexpensive mail order course in the Masters' Meditation. With their continued assistance, we now have an outreach that covers North America, Europe, and several other countries.

Through the media of our extension course, seminars, and books, we are now prepared to offer this meditation and its all-inclusive benefits to everyone. Our spiritual teachers offer it as a method that could save the world.

## Chapter II

### A Troubling Vision

I groped blindly through the darkness into the living room, and dropped down upon the sofa. "Stop making me have those dreams," I yelled to no one in particular. "I need more sleep."

Eyes closed tightly, I stretched out on the sofa, and wrapped myself with an afghan. By that time a string of pictures began flashing one by one through my mind.

Mataji and Mirva had come, sensations of their presence danced all around me.

"You're a wreck," the pictures said.

"More like a nightmare," I replied. "Its not supposed to happen. Can't you do something?"

"You are drifting to sleep," the pictures that were Mataji said. "You will sleep for a little longer. We'll talk later. You are now asleep, now asleep, sleep, sleep."

In almost no time I came awake, feeling good and completely refreshed. The first light of day streamed into the room. I reached over, closed the window and rolled back onto the sofa. Lingering sensations indicating the presence of my two masters remained with me.

"We've told you before," Mataji said, "we are not causing the nightmares."

"I believe you, of course. Are they caused by something I am doing?"

"You are working too hard," she said, but it was you who insisted you still had time to write another book."

"You show me the pictures. All I do is put it down on paper."

"Then let's not waste time," she said. "We show you

now what to cover today."

I like this part the best, I thought. These are the times that I live the scenes that I bring to life on the pages of the book.

These are the Ascended Masters. They are angels that exist at higher levels of vibrations, in another dimension of existence that is much higher than our own.

From our own dimension, I had volunteered to bring their message to earth. That was long ago. Since then, my time has been their time. The pay is not good, but the fringe benefits are out of this world.

Many of them have lived on earth. Through diligent work. they have earned the right to exist at this dimension higher than our own, the angelic realm they originally came from.. They know us well, are concerned for our well being, and help us as much as they can.

Many people have written about these masters, much of it is different from what my teachers have shown me, and I have worked with them almost continuously for well over forty-nine years.

Every scene in this book flows from the minds of those masters. With their help, I teach an extremely powerful meditation and a system of healing that flows to me from their minds.

This book, then, is their book. Look for their guiding hand behind each scene that I describe. You will know it is the product of the mind of one or more of them. Share the excitement that flows to me, and through me to you. It is an effort to bring the possibilities and miracles of this spiritual contact and a powerful meditation to you.

Everything I write is possible, and is attainable by those who live the Masters' Meditation through the home

## Chapter II

study course I make available or teach in person. When you learn the meditation, you will have attained the same contact with the masters that I have. You will also have found your own path, your own destination, your own destiny, your own way of life.

It is offered especially to those who feel their lives are incomplete, despite the promises of man and his many establishments and what they have to offer.

I know that I am asleep, and all of these thoughts flow through a part of me called the superconscious mind. Visions from the masters fill this mind with their messages. Most of them are clear, easily understood. Behind them are other visions that are obtuse like the unclear quatrains of Nostradamus that can have many different meanings.

The disturbing picture passed through my mind again: a playing card depicting the face of death, a tarot card, one of the major arcana, death. In no more than a split second, it flashed past me. Then it was gone.

One picture amid thousands of scenes of beauty and wonder. Only one picture signifying disaster. in sharp contrast to all of the others. Could it have caused the unpleasant dreams that troubled my sleep? Somehow I feel the answer will soon come.

With the assistance of my guides, I have overcome earth's transient temptations and its negativity. Their meditation has taught me to accept what I cannot change, and hold on to the positive and powerful influence of a much higher level of consciousness. The continuing meditation is not static, but leads me into increasingly higher levels that lift my own consciousness and abilities into ever higher levels. Then comes the promise of attaining an even higher level, and with it the ability to make positive changes I could not perform earlier.

I could still feel my guides presence, and their minds following my thoughts. The absence of comment from them indicated tacit agreement on their part.. It usually made me feel good, knowing they remained close when I was awake, and watched over me while I slept. They allow me three good hours of sleep each night, then fill my mind with visions in the half sleep that follows.

Bit by bit, the continuing visions filled my superconsciousness with pictures of a mighty cosmos beyond our understanding. Then came the alluring scenes from another dimension in time and space, the dwelling place of the masters and angels, all part and parcel of that great cosmos.

The pictures show thousands of beautiful planets, well stocked with nature's plenty and waiting for the coming of our species. Sadly, the inhabitants of our own planet are earthbound, its population having nowhere else to go.

From somewhere in these visions came the vague promise that someday, those of us who studied and learned the meditation well, would advance to the level of attaining the world of the masters when we were ready. The benefits from such an accomplishment would be out of this world.

The early morning contact was followed by a personal meditation, taking me again into a massive concentration of the golden mist of Creation. The minds of the masters caused a whirlwind to form within the mist that surrounded me with a wall of golden light just beyond my reach.

The whirlwind continued spinning in circles about me.

## Chapter II

The tornado-like swirling fire surrounded me, and sent shivers of energy and excitement into every part of my body. They told me the golden mist was the presence of God, and it filled every part of space within the Cosmos.

It filled me with a very positive emotion and sensation that originated at the highest level of Creation. Peace and love filled me, healing every facet of my existence. My mind expanded under the guidance of the masters. The healing touch of the Creator flowed within me, and sent that special benefit into every inner location.

The center of the whirlwind reached above and below me, like a massive tunnel of light connecting our world with that of the higher dimensions.

They taught me to attain that swirling mass of energy at the height of that powerful meditation, and to take others to that level and teach them to attain it on their own when they were ready.

As I continued to work with the whirlwind, they taught me to form a smaller personal swirling pattern of light around me that brought me extra energy in all that I had to do in my daily existence. In fact, as I write these lines, I am surrounded by my own personal energy producing whirlwind.

In an earlier book, Cosmic Fire, I told about my first meeting with the angelic master, Mataji, well over forty-five years ago. While on a meditative retreat in a cabin high in the Himalayan Mountains, I awoke one morning to find her seated at my table with breakfast already prepared.

She explained that she was the Custodian of the meditation I studied, and volunteered to teach me. I agreed. and during the classes that followed, we made a mutual promise. She would continue to work with me if I would agree to bring this powerful method to the attention of our world. True to her promise, she has worked with me since that time.

She introduced me to the basic concept of the special whirlwind meditation that first day.

There are many other meditations that constitute The Masters' Meditation. The Cosmic Whirlwind is one of the most powerful. It is an advanced procedure that leads to the highest possible levels of benefits, including the secret power of the universe.

There are other procedures that must be learned as the student prepares for this higher level. Some of them were explained briefly in my earlier book that I mentioned above. Each meditation is a stepping-stone in the eternal quest of the Light. Some of the more powerful will be explained in detail later.

The whirlwind has numerous methods that enrich one's life in many ways. In all of the beginning procedures, the Temple of Lights' meditation becomes the launching platform from which we begin our ascent along the path. The advanced meditations quickly take us into the Cosmic Whirlwind. At that point, the whirlwind takes over, providing, among other things, this whirling tunnel of light, forming the bridge that leads us to the highest levels of Creation.

The whirlwind, with its tunnel of light leading us to Creation, can bypass the near death experience and happily take us across that bridge, and allow us to view the other side, whenever we have mastered the procedure, and wish to view eternity.

The Bridge to Eternity part of the title of this book

means exactly what it proclaims.  The Cosmic Whirlwind is that bridge.  When we begin our study of meditation, we have chosen the only path I know that can lead you back to creation while living a productive life on earth.

The Cosmic Whirlwind will be presented in more detail a little later in the book.  For now, it is sufficient to know that it represents the sixth level of attainment in the home study part of the meditation that I teach.

It exists at two levels.  One is the formal meditation that is a powerful and uplifting experience.  The other is a smaller, personal meditation, just large enough to encircle your body.  You learn to keep it with you in whatever you do, both day and night.

Both levels are important, and each play an important part in the lives of those who learn to use it in almost every part of their daily activities.

Through this book, the masters and angels also wish to acquaint you with the existence of this powerful method and show you how you can learn to practice it on your own.  It fits in perfectly with the fast pace of our lives and brings all of its benefits to help make that life easier and more rewarding.

The Masters' Meditation leads us into contact with the natural conditions found throughout the universe.  It merges perfectly with the style of living now prevailing in the Western World.  For as little as thirty minutes a day, we can enhance every aspect of our lives while enjoying the rapturous ecstasy of this delightful meditation.

The Eastern meditation does not fit the goals we have set for our lives in our own Western World.  Long hours, or days, or even weeks spent in meditative silence puts the Eastern method our of our reach.  You can ill afford the wasted time when you can learn our own Masters' Meditation in a much shorter time. This book will reveal to you the much higher levels of advancement that are available through the masters' method..

## Chapter III

### The Whirlwind

The outline of Argon's majestic mountains towered above. The thinning golden mist of my personal Whirlwind blended into the rays of the setting sun, revealing the massive crystal doorway to the beautiful Temple of Lights, guiding my pathway into the interior.

Mataji and Mirva greeted me as I entered the portals. . Their auras touched my own, their arms linked gently into mine. Walking three abreast, they led me deep into the Temple, to a location they had never taken me before.

No conversation broke the silence. We had worked together for so long none was needed. From a deep meditative sleep, safe in the protective arms of my personal Cosmic Whirlwind, they had brought me in spirit to this location for what—consultation and guidance perhaps. A door opened silently before us, and I knew the purpose of this visit would soon be revealed.

Most of the rooms within the Temple were located inside the crystal mountain, where a combination of rose and golden light illuminated the interiors. This spacious room possessed its own shielded window with an outside view. They allowed me only a few moments to observe the tops of the crystal mountains around us before leading me to a comfortable chair.

Mirva sat just to my right. Mataji pulled up a smaller chair in front. Almost automatically, my mind prepared itself for the sudden flow of pictures into my awareness from their own. In almost fifty years of instructions, no two consultations were ever the same. They often revealed additional information pertaining to past pictures or future plans.. In the vast expanse of the Cosmos, only a minor portion of its wonders could be experienced in a single lifetime. Intuition told me this special meeting would be an important extension of an already familiar subject.

Another whirlwind announced its arrival, filling me with delightful energy as it expanded my mind's reach into wider levels of awareness.

I mentally picked up the pattern of their thoughts even as their minds merged into the pattern of energy of the whirlwind as it dimmed and became smaller.

I thought, "You have taken me into many whirlwinds in the past. This is the most powerful ever. What does it mean?"

The pictures that continued to come into my mind were clear. As they turned into words, it was easy to imagine her thoughts merging them into mine..

She said, "The whirlwind is a gift to humanity. All of the masters who work with you, and others from many parts of the universe, have joined together and created this special whirlwind in the height of the mists of Creation surrounding your world."

"I thought you never intervened."

Her smile became broader. "Unless you ask," she said. "You and enough of your students have asked. They have agreed from earth to keep the vigil. The masters of the universe will do the rest. It has been made permanent. It will remain as long as needed..."

"Thank you."

"All of the world needs it," she continued. "Those who use it and then assist us, will receive greater benefit."

I said. "How can I tell the newer student its benefit?

I had glanced at Mirva. She said, "Mataji and I share

## Chapter III

the same thoughts. Let her finish."

Mataji continued. "You have worn your whirlwind like a shield for over half of your lifetime, even when asleep. You even used it as a vehicle to bring you here tonight.?

"Tonight?" I asked, looking outside at the bright sunlight.

"I said tonight because you came here out of a deep meditative sleep. That same night will remain in your world until we finish and let you return, no matter when that takes place."

No past, no future, only the eternal present, I thought. That takes a lot of understanding. I might as well have said it aloud.

"Exactly," she replied. Like a flash of instant understanding, the purpose of this meeting came into my mind: the time had come to formally release knowledge of the whirlwind's existence to mankind.

Mataji nodded. "That and much more," she said. "Let's consider first your own personal whirlwind. It takes time and effort to create and maintain it. When I revealed it to you that first morning, your ability to learn and begin using it so quickly came as a surprise. Almost no one except Tschen Li ever grasped it so quickly."

"I wish he had shown it to me in the beginning."

"It's so powerful, I have to decide who has reached the level they can properly use it."

"I knew it's importance," I replied. "You have told me something about the others who misused it."

"Not exactly," she said. "It can't be misused. "When someone tries, its power will be lost to them again."

I remembered a recent letter from an advanced

student, reporting on her experiences with the Whirlwind. She described it as fantastic, and spoke of the uplifting vibrations as she followed my voice through the experience. She had dedicated her life to helping others, and told of healings she had performed when there seem to be no hope. She even worked with the terminally ill, using the special energy to assist them through transition.

Then I remembered what the Master Jesus said, "That he who placed his hand upon the plow and turning back, is not worthy of the Kingdom of Heaven." In other words, great spiritual experiences, joy and other rewards come to those who reach this level along the path to enlightenment. The greatest of all joys comes from sharing this knowledge and these experiences with others in need of help. At that level, it would be unthinkable to return to the physical way of life and thought, and lose those blessings.

Mataji had told me of rulers and leaders she had taught in the past. Some tried to keep the high level rewards for their own personal use, and to share the intermediate meditative experiences with those in their own inner circle of power. After that, they gave only the rudimentary teachings to others. They soon lost the ability and contact, and reverted to the physical

A slight nod from Mataji told me she received my thoughts. Her smile indicated that she agreed.

"Now," she said, "let's get on with the real purpose of this visit." My muscles pulled me straight up in the chair.

"There's more?" I asked. Tensing my muscles to suppress the pulsing vibrations like icicles racing up my spine.

"Time to go," she said as she and Mirva stood up.

## Chapter III

My mind automatically tensed to hold beneath the surface of thought a deeper feeling that they were preparing me for something else equally important. In their own time, they would tell me. We were already headed for the door.

Together we walked through a door in the back of the room. One on each side of me. They each took one of my arms as we left the Temple of Lights behind us. We were already floating through the golden mist of Creation, high in the air above the mighty crystal mountains of Argon, a planet used by the Masters and Angels for special meetings and teaching.

Before us stood Astoria, the tallest mountain on the planet, so-called by the masters because it seemed to reach into the lower limits of the stars. We moved to a level area where ragged crystal formations surrounded us, glittering in golden rays of an immense sun located an indeterminate distance behind. Powerful rays of the sun bathed my body, flowing in and filling every atom with liquid sunshine and a special energy carrying with it the promise of everlasting life.

"Why this special treatment?" I wondered, forgetting for a moment the many years they had been with me.

I didn't have to look. Mirva had merely touched a forefinger to the lips. I would wait, or course, until they were ready.

The many special attunements to the crystal consciousness they gave me in the past, made me feel at home in the maze of crystal foundations around us. Dazzling patterns of flickering light dotted the terrain in all directions, extending to the limit of our view. To explore it alone would lead one to become hopelessly lost in a jungle, a maze of haphazardly scattered crystals from which there would be no return without a spiritual guide. The attunements gave me feeling of belonging, but with a healthy respect for its vastness.

Under their guidance, we had moved to a location where glittering, irregularly shaped structures of crystals rose like large houses before us.

We stepped cautiously through an opening into one of the crystal monuments. Although we had space to move into the interior, nothing around us could be called a room. Growing crystal formations like tree limbs in a forest, reached ever-outward, seeking to fill every available space. Nothing below us resembled a floor. Surrounded on all sides by crystal forms, Mataji and Mirva held my arms. We floated in the center of the only available space, a small vortex like the center of the powerful Cosmic Whirlwind.

I stood there amazed. The crystal consciousness manifested strongly within and around me. My old friend, Aliathor, liaison between the crystal consciousness and that of humanity touched my mind in approval as the consciousness of the crystal world flowed into the vortex and began spinning rapidly around me like the Cosmic Whirlwind.

"The crystal consciousness?" my mind asked.

"Exactly," Mataji replied.

"Another meditation?"

"Yes," she said. Her hands felt warm as she held my left arm. "Another reward for those who master the whirlwind."

Another mind moved gently into mine. Mirva now controlled the white and misty golden light spinning

## Chapter III

rapidly around me in a mystical embrace.

Vibrations within me intensified. Every atom of my body tingled as they struggled to accommodate the ever-increasing vibrations. High levels of increasing radiance held me in its arms. The consciousness of Creation surged strongly within, filling me with visions of eternity. A powerful master stood before me.

"The Master Healer?" I asked.

"Yes," Mirva replied. "He always comes with Aliathor and they work together. They are with us now."

"Like in the Crystal Pool," I thought.

Mataji came alive. "Yes," she said. "That was a powerful beginning. "It will all come together in this meditation. We call this the Crystal Transformer. This is where you perfect your personal contact with Universal Knowledge. An awareness of the entire universe."

"With it, Soul travel will be a breeze," I thought.

"Only if we are with you," she said, "but there is more."

"I sensed it a moment ago."

"I put it there."

"Why the mystery?"

"Did you sense that, too?" She asked.

"Yes."

"Your progress continues to amaze me," she said. "You do trust us?"

"If you two told me to jump off a high cliff, I would. Does that answer the question?"

"Don't be ridiculous," she said. "We would never do that."

"I know, tell me about it anyway."

Her voice quivered almost imperceptibly. She said, "In

their wisdom, the special council of masters who work with us knows what will happen in your world, and they want you to have a special experience."

"Something to do with the bad dreams that have come to me lately?" I asked.

She nodded. "Yes," she replied. "Your quick understanding really amazes us."

"I have always worked with them and you."

"They wanted you to be alone. We wouldn't agree unless Mirva and I could be with you."

"You will be with me?"

"Yes."

"And you can't tell me in advance?"

"It would not be as effective."

"Then I agree."

The preliminaries could now be put aside. I had agreed to accompany two spiritual masters on some universal excursion, of such a nature that the time and the destination could not be revealed in advance. The crystal transformer meditation could now continue, but part of my mind would be filled with visions of what was to come.

They brought me here today to familiarize me with that total awareness and contact of the crystal consciousness with the universe, and to notify me of a special experience that would come to me soon.

In addition to Mataji and Mirva, other masters usually assisted me when I taught this meditation. When the two of them took me on a special journey into the universe, I knew it would be an extra special journey. I resolved to remain alert in order to recognize and make the most of it when it occurred.

## Chapter IV

### The Ascension

The final moment came with no warning It .came in an alarming moment of half awake, half asleep sensations. Struggling to remember, I tried to shake away the binding pressure trying to force my mind to retreat into a state of nothingness.

Illusions of thought fought to rise above the tightening pressure. Then came a dim memory of Erna's tear-stained eyes, the agonizing look of concern on her face, and of the biting fumes of rubbing alcohol as she cooled my burning body. Finally came the troubled sleep, much too long after midnight.

But where was I? A rising surge of confusion engulfed me. Soft arms of nothingness embraced me, taking me nowhere and everywhere. The soft mattress still pressed into my burning back while my weightless body floated free above the bed, becoming part of the entire universe. Occupying two locations at one time added to the confusion. If only the entity that set the stage for my departure would finish the job.

If this was death, I had never anticipated its final moment. Time ran out at some time, I knew, but I was too busy, doing the work of the masters, I thought. Surely they would let me finish. Now the strong emotion of an unexpected feeling of reality lay buried in a misty gold and silver light that surrounded me.

A new life force embraced me. It held me in gentle arms of love, and removed the bindings holding body and soul together. I was free at last, but what now? Where did I go from here?

That powerful force of new life and spiritual love had

lifted me into a higher position, just above the bed in which I had been sleeping only moments before. No memory of that ascension remained. My mind told me this was it. No silver cord bound body and soul together. No longer connected, the strongest sensation was that of freedom.

Had I learned any lessons from that past life? Had I earned the right to take those lessons with me and enjoy some extended state of continued awareness? Even in these early moments of separation, there was no desire to reenter the lifeless body, yet some inner urge had me reach below to close the gaping mouth. We were dimensions apart, I could almost touch it, but an unknown force stood in the way.

Although we slept in darkness, a mystical light brightened the room. My body lay just below. The persistent urge to close its mouth remained. An unwelcome part of the memory of death, perhaps. It represented the final act of life. Strangely I had never before considered that it would happen to me.

Erna lay curled on her left side near the edge of the bed, her back to my lifeless body. I remembered she preferred to sleep nearer the center. That nearness always brought me the comfort of her warm presence. A pleasant contrast to the narrow hardness of a seaman's bed, and the lonely nights of sleeping alone for many years while sailing the oceans of the world. I wanted to comfort her, tell her not to worry

She had remained near me most of the day before. I almost never became sick, but what the press called the Beijing Flue caught me by surprise. By bedtime a surprising sickness made me weak. I could hardly walk.

## Chapter IV

Erna held my arm, but even that was not enough. My legs gave way and I had to crawl the remaining distance to the bed. She lifted one arm and one leg onto the bed, helped me up and rolled me over on the soft mattress. She never left my side after that. My final memory of that long night was her tear stained eyes as she knelt beside me.

She looked much smaller now, lying there alone. The I Am that was me no longer inhabited the body there beside her. Concerned only for her, I dreaded her surprise on awakening.

The reverie was interrupted when two beings that could only have been angels stood beside me. The touch of their auras filled me with gentle love. The touch of their hands on my arms sent tingling sensations of energy racing up and down my spine. Although memories of the final picture of life would remain, the loving energy of this new life force gave me no time to look back.

The golden light of Creation had intensified. It stood before me now like a tunnel of light, reaching all the way to eternity, perhaps. They didn't have to tell me, I knew it was time to go. Surrounding forces of energy already propelled me forward and upward. Ascension through the golden mist within the long tunnel had begun.

A misty tunnel of light reached for an interminable distance before us. From its interior I could see no beginning, no end. A misty bridge between dimensions reached from physical to spiritual, from materiality to Creation, from death to everlasting life. Had I learned my lessons? Would I be welcome? The gentle touch of angel's hands, and the reassurance of their presence, allowed my mind to enjoy the surrounding peace.

The tunnel stretched ever onward like an endless

desert highway. It was apparently devoid of life, yet teeming with signs of its presence on all sides. We drifted slowly. The golden hue of the wide walls and arching ceiling and floor, radiated Creation's life and love throughout the misty glow within the tunnel.

We floated endlessly along, aware of the sensation of other living things in the vicinity. Occasionally, I caught a glimpse of what might be a young child. They would appear for only a moment. Could they be Cherubs or celestial spirits attending my passage? Responding to a light pressure of the angelic hand on my right arm, I looked, and the smile on her angel face gave the answer. My ascension was well attended.

Others have written of the near death encounter. They tell of the experience, the separation, the tunnel, and the beautiful light. They also tell of the freedom from cares and worldly obligations, then the knowing that they must return. Then of the return before moving through the doorway leading into everlasting life. The memory triggered another gentle squeeze on my arm. This time the angelic smile gave me no discernible answer.

Like radiant sunshine, the deepening of the intensity of Creation's golden mist signaled our approach. Ahead, in the intensifying radiance of God's light and love, the shining doorway into everlasting life beckoned us to approach.

Another angel stood at the door, and opened it as we approached. A familiar hand took mine, and led me to take my first step into Creation's promised land.

At that moment, many surprises occurred swiftly. The angel ahead of me turned and embraced me. A flowing mantel of God's love wrapped me gently in its arms, while

## Chapter IV

the angels at my side allowed their own love to join that of my own angelic master, Mataji, who had joined me at the correct time, to usher me into the fulfillment of the Promise and the Eternal Presence of God.

Although my Tibetan master continued teaching me from the physical plane, Mataji had been my spiritual master and teacher for nearly fifty years. She taught me alone from that level for the first year. Then another master, who called herself Mirva, joined her. Other masters often helped, but the two of them shared the main burden of my instruction from that moment in time.

Surprise followed surprise. Taking me with them, the three angels lifted gently into the air, and floated gracefully over the green grass of eternity. Finally, we came to rest, seated on a bench in an enclosed area surrounding a cathedral like building without the usual spires and decorative artistry. Instead, it was flooded with rainbow colored beams of radiant light that also arched above and filled the air around us. Mirva, my other teacher waited at the bench. She greeted me warmly. My existence at this high spiritual plane suddenly became complete.

Mataji and Mirva nodded in agreement when I made the simple statement. "I know this is the surprise you promised me earlier. You did your work well, but did you have to put me through that experience to bring me here."

Mataji replied, "We did it to prepare you for the next step."

"I don't understand. I was critically ill. Am I really dead?"

She nodded. "At this moment your physical body is clinically dead," she said. "You don't have to return unless you agree."

"Can't you allow some little spark of life to remain?"

"Yes. It is still there, although no one on earth can detect it. You can go back whenever you wish."

"We made a promise nearly 50 years ago. It changed my life."

She nodded.

"I agreed to work with the masters," I said. "Since that time, they have provided for my needs, and I have never looked back."

"Are you satisfied with your progress?"

My heightened awareness at this level of consciousness surprised me. With it came knowledge and feelings of oneness with this location and its people. The barrier separating our lives no longer stood in the way. I was with them in reality. I could clearly sense their physical presence, even touch them. The special feeling of Mirva sitting beside me at my left, of Mataji on my right, and of the two angels standing just in front radiated sensations of nearness and belonging. I was at home and at peace.

Choosing my words carefully, I answered, "With my own personal progress, yes. I have made some headway with my teaching, but still have a long way to go."

"You are aware that our power and influence is limited on the earth plane? Hardening facial muscles wrinkled the smoothness of her face.

"Yes," I said. "By some Divine decree, man has free will. Most of them go to extremes to use that freedom unwisely."

She nodded. "It's only a question of time. Here we coexist in the full energy and splendor of the Eternal

## Chapter IV

Presence. The eternal presence is also the eternal present. There can be no measure of what you call time. With us, that is nonexistent. As time passes back on earth, the physical ages and withers away. Under those conditions, death is inevitable.

"With your Soul and your Mind, which are part of Creation, of the Creator," she continued, "the phenomenon you call death is impossible. The Soul, as part of eternity, outlasts the body, then leaves it when it can no longer function properly."

"Tell me what happens then?" I asked.

"After your soul leaves its body, it finds another after a suitable period of study on a higher plane of existence. Then life goes on as before, where other lessons are learned. Or, you can return to this level permanently."

"This level?"

"Yes," she said, "And we plan to let you see some of the special locations."

"I do want to go back to earth for a little while longer, if it is possible," I said. "My teachings are beginning to attract the attention of people who can make a difference and help bring others into the Light."

"The masters are pleased that you want to go back," she said. "Remember, you have the same right to free will as the others. After nearly 50 years of working with them and us, you could stay here now and claim your right to be one of us.

"Am I ready for that?"

"Your mastership of the Cosmic Whirlwind says yes," She replied. "You sleep in its arms for comfort and protection, it surrounds you in almost every waking moment, you wear it like a garment and a shield."

"And I teach it to everyone who studies your meditation with me."

"Then it's settled," she said. "We will take you through other experiences at this level, then you can go back before you are missed. Don't forget the timelessness of this location. No matter how long you remain here, you will return within minutes of the time that you left"

Nodding in acceptance. I said, "Thank you."

We remained seated on the bench where they had taken me a few moments after our arrival. Small groups of people occasionally entered or left the open doorway of the building in front of us. I somehow knew we would soon enter that door for my own orientation.

There was no congestion, no clutter. Sensations of peace, love and belonging filled me with impressions of a vacation that needed never come to an end, yet leaving moments of the uncertainty of not knowing what was coming next.

Mataji's hand found mine for only a moment. A gentle squeeze of reassurance made everything all right.

## Chapter V

### The Cosmos

Two masters and two angels led me toward the large building. I reasoned it was a meeting place, an orientation and indoctrination center for new arrivals, and for whatever else that was required.

My two guides usually received my thoughts as quickly as they came into my mind. This time there was no response from them or the two angels that walked ahead of us.

Another angel or a guide appeared in the doorway as we ascended the steps. "Meet your instructor," Mataji said simply, as we reached the top step.

No name, no designation of position was given. Tall, confident, wearing a glistening white robe, he nodded in recognition, then led us into the building and into a spacious room. No one other than ourselves was present.

Several chairs indicated it was used as a reception area, but no one sat down. Still standing, they gathered around me in an open area. The instructor stood close to me in front.

The white robe worn by masters and angels is a manifestation of light. They are spiritual beings of light. As expressions of the highest levels of vibrations, they exist in a dimension of unlimited time and space they call the Angelic Realm. Surrounded and filled with uplifting vibrations of energy and love from above, they exist in perpetual contact of the Eternal Presence of God.

My mind flashed back to our earthly existence, and with it to the somber realization of our limited pleasures when compared to those of this level. Then I remembered that two of the angles standing at my side had introduced me to the Masters' Meditation.

That special meditation made the difference. Unlike the others, it always lifted the student's vibrations to the highest levels. It had made this ascension possible, and with it came the promise that those who persevere will be welcomed to this Angelic Realm when they are ready.

One might expect to find a sameness in a world where everyone wears white, yet the opposite is true. Each one possesses a distinct personality and state of being. Even at lower levels of vibration, the meditator learns to recognize special sensations and feelings. For the beginner, when the masters and angels may not be visible, as in meditation or special events, you may not be able to see their form, but sensations and feelings tell you that a master or an angel is still present.

In extremely high level experiences such as this, we see, feel, and communicate easily. Other differences in my own body manifested strongly in my consciousness. With a simple thought, I could increase or decrease the density of my body and adjust its relationship to the gravity of the planet.

Even when surrounded and filled with the astounding revelations of continuing miracles happening all around me, I impulsively allowed one thought of increasing lightness to flow into my mind. As my body began to rise out of the midst of the angels, Mataji grabbed my hand and pulled me back to solid footing.

I sensed a chuckle in her voice that belied the serious frown on her face. She said, "Allow the automatic control to continue as before. There will be time for play later."

I knew the others were aware of what I did, but they showed no indication of disapproval.

## Chapter V

We stood together in a small group, almost touching each other. Differing sensations marked the presence of each of the four beings who had brought me to this level. I knew them perfectly, the energy and pattern of their being reached out toward me, to touch and become part of me. Their dedication to help me reach this higher goal manifested strongly from their minds into mine.

A stronger sensation of my new instructor's presence reached into my mind, impressing feelings of his special abilities and patterns of his personality deep within me. As he drew closer to the combined presence of my special group which surrounded me, the strongest feeling of his presence was spiritual love and compassion for humanity.

Beyond that came the manifestation of a powerful mind that maintained an extremely close relationship with every aspect of Creation. His personal area of responsibility was universal, his power dynamic and unlimited.

Feelings of the Creator's great love for humanity surged stronger as the minds of the others merged with the pure mind of this special angel. Like a holy fire, it all blended together, surrounded my mind, lifted it and my consciousness to levels never before imagined.

We were surrounded by an array of varicolored lights. With multiple colors, beams of light flickered and danced around us. They filled the room with brilliant colors that blended into a rosy golden hue, embracing our group as we stood entranced in the center of the room.

My eyes closed as the room grew brighter. My inner consciousness enabled me to perceive everything in and around us with equal or greater clarity. They often told me that meditation would one day teach me to know and see with my mind. With their help now, it made that special benefit possible.

A golden sun surrounded us, and wrapped us tightly in its arms. Patterns of light gathered us together until the angels' bodies touched and merged more closely with mine. The energy of our group merged as we became one. Our minds as one mind, we became the sum of all there was.

The universe reached out as far as our mind could conceive. That composite mind knew all there was to know. We were the universe, the cosmos. All that was, we were. The others knew. To enable me to see for myself, they allowed the composite mind of all to become my own.

Before me lay billions of galaxies similar to our Milky Way, most of them larger than our own.. Each galaxy consisted of billions of suns, and planets similar to earth. They existed in an array of limitless quantities making even an estimate of their number impossible. They were present in such numbers the human mind could not even grasp the magnitude.

Many planets were already inhabited while others waited for us to grow up and claim our birthright. Then I knew. In the full harmony of the composite mind, I understood why humanity blindly chose to remain earth bound rather than fly with the angels and enjoy the bliss of everlasting life. Almost every facet of life on earth contributed to total immersion in its baser pleasures. The spiritual life was little understood or desired.

For this, humanity paid a terrible price—DEATH. From the knowledge that poured into my superconscious mind from all around me, and from what I had learned

## Chapter V

from contact with the Masters, those of us who followed the Path back to Creation could take one final step from that Path and into everlasting life.

Mataji had promised me earlier that I could remain here now if I wished, but I wanted to return and continue teaching. Here in the rapture and all knowingness of this beautiful land, the perfection of freedom of spirit, and the intimate contact with all knowledge of the universe, gave promise of a lifetime of creative pursuits. With the unlimited supply of creative tools available, everlasting life teemed with creative possibilities.

Something within my spirit seemed to say, make the most of this moment of complete contact with this world of the angels and the masters. The great love of the Creator for us all held me warmly in Its arms, allowed me to merge with the rapture of everlasting life.

Totally merged with five powerful angels, they let me view Creation with a clarity of vision available only to those from whose eyes the scales of earth's blindness had been removed.

The golden mist of the Creator's Eternal Presence lay beautifully within the voids existing between the suns, moons, stars and planets within each galaxy, then extending outward between galaxies and beyond to some unseen infinity.

Within the thousands of views of the mighty cosmos flashing constantly past my super vision, came a reminder from the angels that they had brought me to this level and continued to guide me on this journey. These spectacular views of the reality of Eternity can be experienced by those who study the Masters' Meditation with me. This promise made me feel happy that I had asked Mataji to allow me go back and continue teaching.

The vastness of the cosmos continued to hold me in its spell. The frequency of the presentation slowed. One by one, existing worlds came into my vision. Each gleaming brilliantly like jewels in the sky, their land masses in differing patterns and locations, their lustrous oceans in different shades of blue.

As each world now drifted slowly before my expanded vision, many displayed no evidence of human habitation. In full bloom, fully developed, its trees and vines filled with ripened fruit and vegetables, waiting to be harvested. The only sign of life were bees and butterflies pollinating the blooms, preparing for future harvests that would wither away with no one present to enjoy its generosity.

The inhabited planets appeared much the same as the others. Dotted here and there with small settlements of modest homes that were situated in areas of natural beauty and plentiful harvests. Harvests that occurred naturally, with no other requirement than our hands to gather it and partake of its bounty.

Only one or two small cities showed evidence of the intrusion of man. The natural order of the original planet remained undisturbed.

Our own planet earth moved past my vision, identified by the familiar shape of its continents. Then they pictured the dark side for a special reason, to show me mankind's intrusion into the planet's natural order. The continents were literally dotted with lights, almost from pole to pole, showing humanity's congested presence in almost every habitable location.

From somewhere within the composite mind around me came the disturbing suggestion, that earth's population

## Chapter V

suffered under a quarantine of its own making. Why else would we exist under such contamination and congestion with the paradise of so many earth like planets waiting for our coming?

The mind that I recognized above the others could only be that of my own master, Mataji. She said, "The only way out of that prison alive is this. Why do you think we have spent most of your lifetime teaching you our method, and helping you teach it to the world?"

When I tried to reply, there was no answer. My mind was the sum of the composite mind again. The pictures continued to flash past my vision.

For a moment I remembered what the masters had told me about soul travel. They said that in the Masters' Meditation, one could only experience a limited number of visitations to other parts of the universe in one lifetime on earth. Now, after this near death experience, it appears that our students having advanced to that level could begin learning about these other universes in what they call everlasting life.

Until now, I had studied with the masters for nearly fifty years. For thirty-two years I held responsible positions in the business world, and studied meditation and philosophy with the masters. The positions that I held made it easy to devote some of my work time and most of my off time to the masters' studies.

During that time, they had shown me many of the scenes displayed in the pictures that now appeared before me. The difference between then and now was clarity. While in meditation, the pictures came as if in a dream or a vision. Now they came to me as big as life, and with the total clarity of reality. What a magnificent view!

In meditation, they had taken me to communities of glistening crystal buildings, where humans of several advanced levels worked in harmony on communal projects. I had the privilege to study special subjects in some of their universities. Degrees are awarded for work completed. Not many from earth are able to view these awards, although they will exist for an eternity scribed in the annals of what some call the Akashic Records.

They were now showing me the crystal city located on a planet of a distant galaxy where I once witnessed the construction of a large spaceship destined to carry the emigrants to planet earth millions of years ago.

The words, destination Lemuria, flashed in my mind, but that was a long time in the past. Now, as the scenes shifted to other planets, I understood why that revelation was confusing to me then, but I still had a lot to learn.

Until now, the mind of my Heavenly Instructor pulled the strings. That is, with the assistance of my masters, his powerful mind enabled our composite mind to view the vast expanse of the cosmos. He had also arranged the display of the pictures depicting its content.

We also maintained the total fusion of our minds and bodies that enabled us to function as an expanded super-consciousness. His mind now directed itself to me in particular. Of course, the others in our group received his thoughts and instructions to me.

He said, "I have followed your progress from the instant Master Joshua made contact with you when you were very young. We were all pleased when you lived out your time as a young child, yet followed the advice of your master in the matters of temptations that could have caused you trouble and led to heartaches that could retard

## Chapter V

your advancement.

"Knowing of your promise to learn and teach our meditation, and pleased with your progress as a young man, many masters and angels watched over you during your involuntary participation in that awful World War II. Although you knew nothing of us at the time, we made sure you were aware that someone up Here was looking after you.

"Even others around you seemed aware that you led what they called a charmed life. You once stated that you had so many so-called buddies it made you a little nervous. You could think of no reason for your popularity. If you remember, they accepted you completely when you were promoted to captain of an ocean liner at a very young age. It was no accident that it happened when only you could take advantage of the opportunity.

"We guided you to begin the study of our meditation when your age was the same as the Master Jesus when he began his ministry. On earth, that is the best age to begin serious lifetime responsibilities.

"After the long period of your apprenticeship, we allowed you to begin teaching. The information you have just received is a new beginning. We will now allow your top students admission to this same location. You can bring them here, then allow their own masters to show them any part of Creation they have acquired the ability to examine for themselves."

He had paused for a moment. Quivering from the excitement, I had to ask, "How do I get them through the death experience in order to come?"

The sensation of a happy smile flowing through the

composite mind made me feel good. He said, "Simply use the Cosmic Whirlwind. It is the bridge to eternity, the tunnel leading from earth to Heaven. When they are ready, take them into the whirlwind with the masters."

"One more question," I said. "Do we really have to die to come to this paradise?"

The angels answered in unison, "No. Many of us maintain an earthly connection, but spend most of our existence here to recover from earth's negativity."

The supreme mind of the instructor came alive. He said, "You teach meditation to others under the guidance of your two special masters. Other masters assist when you work with larger groups. Mataji and Mirva are special angels, closer than your own family. They have volunteered to be with you throughout this special assignment. After that, they will be your spiritual companions in other things you will feel worth while at that time.

"You will return to your present life and continue your work. The illness that brought you here was the natural result of a visit you made to a sick friend. You did not sanitize yourself soon enough when you returned home.

"One more thing before I leave. You will be brought here many times in the future for instruction. The four angels with you now will bring you. More often than not I will join you, If not, the four of them are quite capable of teaching you what you need to know.

"I leave you now in their capable hands."

His withdrawal from our midst came slowly, like losing part of your own self. The energy of the other four angels began to fill the gap left by his departure. The joint energy of their beings had lifted me to extreme levels of awareness.

## Chapter V

My mind didn't want to descend from such a lofty mental contact. The total fusion of our bodies slowly faded away, but the sensation of unity remained. We were destined to remain a single unit with a single purpose, teaching others at that location was an easy way back to Creation.

Mataji answered for the group. "This will be our meeting place whenever we bring you here," she said.

The four of them pulled up chairs, and we sat close together in a semicircle. Mirva smiled, and I knew she would have more to say before we went back.

Every beautiful Masters' Meditation leads the participant into such a high level of spiritual contact that it remains with them for several days thereafter. Those who meditate daily, live the meditative high experiences almost continuously.

Nothing I had ever experienced could ever compare with the total contact with Creation that had just ended. Whirling winds of spiritual ecstasy continued to spin rapidly around me, leaving invigorating vibrations in every part of my body. I knew that it would be my destiny to never return to a normal state of consciousness again.

Borne on wings of an ocean of golden light, I floated amid surging beams of soft blue, violet, and white light tinged with gold. Amid sensations of ecstasy and peace, the joyous feeling of God's love overlaid the enraptured terrain. I would never be the same again.

Mataji said, "It's time for you to return to your home where you will sleep well in what remains of the night. Mirva has allowed a deep and peaceful sleep to come upon both you and your wife. In the morning, you will feel better.

The feeling of joy and peace surrounding me at that time, lifted me into such a high state of rapture, I could think of nothing that would make me feel any better.

The life after death experience had come to a close. I felt wonderful.

## Chapter VI

### The Awakening

Thanks to Mirva's sleep inducing magic, we slept well for the remainder of the night, and awakened at our usual hour. Erna quietly got up, and after a few moments came over to my side of the bed. The tingling sensation of her energy touched me gently. She just stood there. When she detected my even breathing, an almost inaudible sigh indicated relief.

Still half asleep, I welcomed her concern as I lay quietly, not wishing to awaken fully at that moment. So much had happened, I needed more time to adjust to the memories of the night before and put it all together. Apparently satisfied, Erna left the room. I needed extra time to adjust to the physical mode of existence.

Standing beside the bed, I tested my body's reflexes. I felt good. Energy from last night's visit to the higher levels of Creation had restored my body to its usual sense of well being. A little later, fully dressed, I entered the living room and said good morning to a surprised Erna.

It was good to see her smile as she looked me over with her usual care. She even gave my shoulder a little push, and laughed at my strength to resist. Satisfied, she got me our one cup of our special coffee for the day, and we sat down in our usual chairs.

"You recovered quickly," she said. "You were asleep when I finally let go and went to bed last night. I had done all I knew how, and turned it over to the masters and to God. I was fully prepared to find you dead this morning. I don't even have to ask how you feel, your face and actions tell me."

"You know how ill I was last night," I said. "Well,

after you finally went to bed, Mataji and Mirva came to me in a beautiful vision, and healed me. And they did a whole lot more."

Something in her voice made me look closer. She dabbed her eyes with a tissue, but the smile framing her face made me feel good. She said, "Where were they last night when we needed them? I prayed, and begged them to come. Most of the time when I ask, they usually come rather quickly."

"They were with us every moment," I said. "Perhaps most of their energy was directed to me. I felt their touch through the entire ordeal. I believe that in your intense concern and anxiety, you expected their presence to be something more powerful."

Even as I told her the story, and for a time afterwards, she sat quietly. She had been with me in the meditation for over ten years. We worked together in that and also with the healing method that flowed from the energy that accompanied it. It pleased me when she accepted it as part of her own life, as it had been a part of me for so many years.

She showed no surprise when I told her that Mataji and Mirva met me as I entered the Angelic Realm, but raised questions about the two angels that met me at the beginning of the near death experience and guided me up through the tunnel of light.

"You said that you thought you knew them," she said. "What made you think that?"

"They reminded me of someone I thought I knew."

"Whom did they remind you of?"

"Our two joy guides. "

She said, "We have both agreed they could be masters

## Chapter VI

or angels. They only play the part of joy guides. Wait a moment and I'll find out."

She went into her room, leaving me to sit quietly and think. She needed privacy to communicate with her guides. When she returned, the broad smile on her face gave me the answer.

She said, "You made the right assumption. They were with you all the way. They said something else that came as a surprise, their participation was not part of the plan. In fact, I think they had to insist quite strongly before they were allowed to do it."

"Mataji and Mirva had to do the same thing," I said. "Other masters from the special council would have done just as well. I knew and found contentment in my own spiritual family. In something as serious as death, no one else could have made me feel quite as comfortable as their presence.

That reminded me of the time, only a few days earlier, when Mataji told me the masters planned to take me on a special trip, an adventure that I had to take blindly, not knowing when it would occur or where they planned to take me. Neither she nor Mirva would agree if they could not go with me. Our joy guides took the same position. Now I knew that the near death experience of the night before had been that plan.

Finding my own spiritual family became one of the most beautiful gifts flowing from meditating with the masters. The spiritual masters who were my guides and teachers, had made their presence a part of my life from early childhood. Contact with them blossomed dramatically into ever-increasing spiritual experiences and light. It began in the surprise of an unexpected revelation that grew slowly into the most important part of my life.

Most people fear death, and hang on to life as long as they can. The fear seems to come from the belief that termination of everything comes with death. You only have one chance at life, and that is all.

It was not until Tschen Li began teaching me the Masters' Meditation that I found reincarnation to be a possibility. When the masters began to teach it as truth, and from what I observed in the lives of the ascended masters, reincarnation slowly became the only explanation of the continued existence of the soul in this and all other dimensions of existence.

The continuing existence of the soul puzzled me in the beginning of this study. From what others in their self-assumed authority had always said, the masters, angels and guides were separate entities, each having its own higher level of existence and each separate from the other.

In that poorly understood concept of existence, man existed as an outcast. He enjoyed the transient pleasures of earthly existence, but suffered the interminable pain that came as the natural consequence of such a belief and in humanity's separation from Creation.

With the acquisition of meditation's universal knowledge came the understanding that humanity's passing fling with the interim pleasures of earth could at best be only temporary. With it came the promise of immortality and the eternal existence of the soul. It had been there all the time. Meditation beckoned from the open door into Creation's everlasting life.

Each meditation took me into more highly developed levels of existence, and into other dimensions of reality. Last night's near death experience could have been a

## Chapter VI

reality. I was actually there in person, in a little lighter physical body than usual. The intense feelings of joy and ecstasy surged through me as I floated through the air with ease. The deep feeling of rapture continued to dance around me and fill me with sensations of nearness to everlasting life.

When at the height of this experience, Mataji advised me I could remain there forever, my heart leaped with joy. The promise of living in the bliss and freedom from stress found in that location, made my every dream of eternal life come true. I could scarcely believe my own words when I asked to return to earth.

My long years of study with these spiritual messengers of the Creator filled my life on earth with unanticipated. joy. Great rewards came to me as I taught it to others, and I wanted to continue my work until we created another qualified teacher.

It made Erna happy when I told her my decision. She had been helping me teach for more than four years, and knew more about the process than anyone else. I wanted her to accept the mantel of Teacher freely, and felt that she needed more time to make up her mind. Under the guidance of our masters, anything could happen.

Recently she made a statement that revealed the height of her spiritual advancement. She said the lessons she had learned from the meditation had brought her to the point that she no longer feared death. My experience of the night before had shown me the true nature of death or transition. That which is the real you, the soul and the mind, moved easily back and forth within and in between lifetimes.

My Tibetan master, Tschen Li, taught me a valuable

lesson in this regard. I think of almost all of the people I know suffering the many forms of ill health that resulted from the pace of today's style of living. Then I contrast that with Tschen Li's sound mind and robust health while vigorously pursuing his daily work from an advanced age that exceeded the century mark.

That was his age at the beginning of our relationship, He continued teaching me for over 32 years. He spoke very little on that subject at the beginning. Near the end of our earthly association, when I mentioned that he didn't look a day older, he said that this meditation led his footsteps along the path to longevity.

That fascinating possibility that meditating with the masters could somehow assist in attaining a long and healthy life slipped easily into the forefront of my mind. Tschen Li lived an extraordinarily long and productive life. He mastered this meditation as a child. Then he accepted the wonderful changes that came to his life through its continued practice. He lived according to its principles. When he was ready, he ascended to the higher angelic level to be with the ascended masters.

Then came the realization that a change in the pattern of my own thinking had also occurred. Like a tiny pebble in the shoe, it only pained a little. One knew it was there, but when the mind is filled with other things, it remained in the background, scarcely noticed.

The change had occurred last night, during the intense attunement process with the angels. Total contact with the great Cosmic Consciousness became clearer. One by one, barriers to the unlimited storehouse of information called Universal Knowledge came down.

Here, at the height of my meditative experience with

## Chapter VI

the masters, I had found the way back to the knowledge humanity had lost somewhere in the distant past, near the beginning of life on this planet.

Contact with that knowledge came to me during the expanded moments when under the guidance of angels, my own mind soared freely over the vast expanse of the Cosmos. All of Creation lay before me, there for my use as well as others who had attained this height. There seemed to be no beginning or end to Its unlimited domain.

Four of the angels guiding me on this journey were ascended masters, part of my own spiritual family. At this level, connection between our minds became total. As I looked into the awesome mind of Creation, each mind of the individuals comprising that mind lay bare, open to the scrutiny of others should one care to look. With each mind in total contact with the entire body of knowledge that was the Cosmic Consciousness, no one participating cared to examine the inner thoughts of those who shared that knowledge with them.

Look back and bring into your present memory the most intense moment of rapture and joy you have ever experienced. See and feel it multiplied many thousands of times. Add the purity of the angels to that intense feeling of God's love, and you will have an idea of the eternal bliss that awaits those who attain this level.

When you live in eternal contact with that love, when the entire physical content of the universe is at your disposal, when there are no boundaries blocking your path to wherever you wish to travel, you then choose your own journey through that level of existence based on your own choice logically selected by your then powerful mind.

From your now present level of development, it would

be impossible to know or to even make judgment on what you would then decide.

Every person on earth is a potential beneficiary of the open road to eternity so many of the advanced students of this meditation have attained. When they find it, after lifting their consciousness to that level, they begin to share it with as many others as they possibly can. When you reach that summit, you are not alone. Saints, peasants and others from the ancient past will share your abode, all asking but one thing from life: to follow that sacred path to eternity and to dwell there in peace forever.

What a worthwhile project that is for any soul seeking to find its way back to Creation.

These are some of the memories that followed me from out of the death experience. After only a brief look into eternity and the everlasting life of those who have attained it, life on earth could never be the same again.

Prior to that brief taste of everlasting life, I had shared my existence with ascended masters. I set out to become the teacher of a beautiful meditation, and discovered that it was the story of their own lives. Not only was it far-reaching and powerful, but the key to eternity and everlasting life and the method for attaining it

As I continued to teach their meditation, more and more students would be reaching the higher levels. Many of that group are like me, seeking to attain the highest pinnacle they can reach.

The masters promised to assist me in taking them to the same level they took me. When they said that this time, we would use Cosmic Whirlwind to get there, I breathed a breath of relief.

We will learn more about the Cosmic Whirlwind later.

## Chapter VII

### Ascension Revisited

We had agreed that the special location would be our general meeting place. The building, and the room from which they had shown me the expanded vision of eternity loomed into my vision, even as my body lay in my bed at home, half asleep. The minds of Mataji and Mirva my two special masters, gently touched my own. I arrived in the room a few moments later to find them waiting.

They were seated about a foot apart, with an empty chair facing them in front of me. A thought filtered through my mind. "I wonder if this will be our customary method of contact in the future?" I asked.

As usual, they knew what I had thought. Mataji said, "Yes, but have you noticed anything new?"

Looking around me in amazement, I said, "Yes. Everything is so clear and real."

With the exception of the times she had materialized on earth in my presence to teach me special lessons, the clarity of the location and of their presence now, had changed to absolute reality.

Although we existed in a very high level of spiritual awareness, the feeling of their hands, as I reached out and touched them, was real. Mataji smiled. Again she had understood my brief thought. Mirva nodded in agreement.

Mataji continued, "The angel, your special instructor, who took you and us on your tour of the Cosmos yesterday, has already taken his report of you and your progress to the members of a special council who monitor earth . In their wisdom and perfect understanding of what is happening in your world, they have decided to allow your work to proceed at a much faster pace."

I looked from one to the other. Directing my words to both of them, I said, "You are with me every time that I teach. You know my daily schedule. Tell me how to find time for anything else."

Mataji's understanding made me feel a lot better., "Working together," she said, "we'll find a way."

Her first question had indicated the existence of something new. To me, the most noticeable improvement appeared in the clarity. Instead of seeing the location from the dream state as before, it was now clear and almost real. When I had touched their hands, the reality told me I was here in person and not in a dream.

We no longer communicated in pictures only. The actual words also appeared in my mind as the angels communicated. Beyond that, my mind was more clearly attuned to many things happening around me.

Mataji had followed my thoughts. She agreed by saying, "Exactly." Then she continued, "They foresee that many of your students will soon reach new levels, and be ready to come to this location for their own advancement. You, of course, will bring them to this level. You will need extra training in order to teach them properly."

"How will I find the time?" I asked.

She said. "We will bring you here while you sleep."

Despite the vast amount of knowledge yesterday's experience had afforded me, I knew it would take time to sort it out in my mind. Then I could put it to use. I could feel their minds linked closely to mine as they followed the train of thought flowing through my own.

"Thank you," my mind said to both of them. "I understand it a lot better."

I knew this new level of teaching could only happen

## Chapter VII

as the result of the long years of study and contact with these angelic masters. For many years, their contact with me had come in the form of visions while I was half asleep. The experience of that contact detracted from the quality of a full night's sleep. The added energy from them helped, but not completely.

The fusion of the minds of the angels with mine, had lifted me another level nearer in my quest on the path back to Creation. Two benefits flowed from this contact. First, as Mataji had promised, they would bring me here. That would allow my physical body to enjoy a peaceful sleep, with my mind at this level, remaining here as long as they wished. Second, we were no longer governed by time as measured on earth. At this level, time does not exist. A teaching session here could be for any length of time. Whatever amount of time elapsed, I would awaken at my usual time the following morning, aware of the incident but fully refreshed and ready for my usual day's activities.

Mataji and Mirva had followed my thoughts. Mirva said, "You now understand this teaching process."

Their two minds embraced my own. The picture that followed was that of a couple in their early thirties. In the knowledge that followed filled my expanded mind. The entire sequence of events they wanted me to witness came instantly into my superconscious mind. As if in a trance, I saw the entire picture. The names of the participants were unimportant. What they wanted me to learn came to me in that same split second of eternity.

Like many younger people of our own era, their concerns centered on the present and their own self-gratification. Both worked, but the return from their labor never paid the bills. Believing they could not afford to have children, they made sure that it never happened. They quarreled often. Their marriage continued to deteriorate.

They lived with the girl's father, saw to his meager needs, but took his small social security check to help with expenses. He lived in his own modest home. With no money, his only purchase was medication given to him by Medicaid.

Someone had given his daughter one of my meditation tapes. In the frustration of her life, she couldn't bring herself even to concentrate on the one thing that could have given her the help she needed. The tape lay on her night table, unused until one night it feel to the floor. She had long forgotten, and never thought of it again.

Her father picked it up as he straightened up her room the next day. That afternoon, prior to his nap. he listened to the tape for the first time. It changed his life.

I even heard my voice on the tape as he listened. The Temple of Lights meditation brought the listener into total contact with the inner world, into total recognition and contact with that person's own masters, and into contact with the Cosmic Consciousness.

They allowed me to sense the father's total immersion in the spiritual energy and higher levels of consciousness he experienced. The rapture of the meditation carried him into the heights of blissful contact with Creation, and into the knowingness of All.

The two angels that brought me to this, the total light of Eternity yesterday, guided him through his first session. His own masters appeared at the correct time. At the proper moment, he saw their faces and they give him their names. His contact with them intensified with each passing moment, and they accepted the responsibility for his guidance.

From the moment of his first meditation, he knew he had found his Path, the road back to Creation he had so vainly sought for an entire lifetime. His one meditation tape had been exposed to light, dust and humidity for so long it soon became unusable.

In his intense concentration on the tapes as he meditated, he quickly memorized them. After that, he needed only see the pictures in his mind. With the aid of his own masters, he could enter into a deep meditation on his own, any time he wished.

He meditated at least three times daily. His health improved, his strength returned, but he wisely concealed the improvement from his daughter. In the period of silence after each meditation, he prayed for more instructions. His masters asked mine for help.

It amazed me to see how they helped. They allowed him to tune in and hear my voice giving one of the meditations. Then they would repeat that meditation to him for a few days. He quickly learned the pictures described by my words, and worked with them on his own as he did the first tape. Step by step, they took him through the series of tapes that led him to an extremely high level of contact.

What followed amazed me even more. He had become fully regenerated, and something more. In the high level of spiritual contact and guidance he had attained, his masters had given him complete understanding of the world around him and ideas how to improve it.

One morning he walked into the business office of the firm from which he was forced to retire because of ill health a few years earlier. Amazed at his new look and appearance, the office workers greeted him warmly. A secretary took him in to see the president, who took him for a tour of the plant, then to his club for lunch.

During the course of the lunch, the president asked his opinion of the plant operation. He agreed when the man said that it hadn't changed at all since he left. In confidence he learned that was also the concern of the president. When asked if he knew the reason, the man confided that as the company accountant, he always gave the production manager up to date data, and even made suggestions for improved production. His host said that the last few years of the man's service were the most productive. When he left, productivity slowed down.

At that moment, the picture they wanted me to see became clear. The production manager took the credit for the increased productivity that came as the result of the man's suggestion. The man, advancing in age and already in ill health, had a heart attack during the period of frustration that followed and was retired without pension since he needed more service to qualify.

At that point the man informed the president that he knew how to improve output even more. I could see he had worked on the production plan for years, and during the meditation some of the information coming into his mind had given him the improvements he had just suggested.

The final result, he is back to work in a better job that allowed him to move from his old location. His life now complete, he is looking to the final fulfillment of his life's destiny.

The last picture showed his daughter and her husband

## Chapter VII

continuing their hopeless life style, unaware of the miracle that occurred around them. The daughter's unconcern about her father's location disturbed me, Then I saw some concern in her mind after the social security check stopped, and a single thought that perhaps he had checked himself into an old age home. Beyond that, her lack of concern for him continued. She made no further effort to locate him.

He had simply rented an apartment near his place of employment. Full of energy, his health restored, he pursued the many opportunities coming to him out of his meditations. Happy for the first time in years, he released the past and never looked back.

The story came to an end when the pictures stopped flowing in my mind. My angelic masters slowly materialized in the space before me, still seated in their chairs. In my mind, I sent them the thought, "Why do I believe that story actually happened?"

Mataji replied, "It did."

"I have no memory of it."

"We told you for a reason," she said. "You have many students, is that correct?"

"Yes," I said. "In some states, a few foreign countries."

"We knew that, of course," she said. "Most of them you have never seen. Beyond those you personally teach, there are many who have attained high levels of advancement, and are also teaching others.

"We just showed you one happy ending that you knew nothing about, and there are many others similar to that. It is possible you will never know, but that is not as important to you as is the knowledge that you did it.

What you helped us begin on earth is succeeding, and that is only the beginning."

"I don't understand . . .."

"Let me finish," Mataji said. "For a little while, you will meet us almost nightly at this location. We have much work to do. Mirva and I, along with others who will come with us occasionally, will teach you here or in other locations at this level. We will prepare you to bring others to this location, to see the land where they will live during the hereafter, and to meet and mingle with those who have attained everlasting life."

At loss for words, my mind sent me a picture. "All of this from a simple meditation."

Mataji and Mirva simply moved their heads slowly from side to side. They heard and understood, of course. Their minds embraced mine again. Realization of the present slowly faded, replaced by pictures flowing through my mind. The flow of words accompanying the pictures became intense.

"Each night you join us in this location," they said, "will encompass one intense subject. The next session will be a discussion of The Cosmic Whirlwind, its past, present, and how we intend to use it in the future.

"This is important for your own understanding, and for those who read your book.

"We return you to your own bed now, and be with you and your students in tomorrow's meditation."

I tried to say good-bye from the depth of sleep. The next memory was that of the morning sunshine on the window sill.

## Chapter VIII

### The Cosmic Whirlwind

As they had promised, Mataji and Mirva called me again from a deep sleep. Seated in the same chairs, they waited in the special room of the Angelic Realm as before. A smile and a brief nod completed their greeting as I sat down in the chair already centered in front of them.

The welcoming touch of their hands reminded me that under the advanced training given me in this location, the reality of our contact was more nearly perfect than in the dreamlike experience of meditation. The intense joy felt in the spiritual contact now continued within me. Creation's unconditional love wrapped me in its arms.

Although my body seemed to be solid, sensations of lightness gave me the feeling that with one thought, I could fly.

"Come on back down," I heard in my mind, "and let's get to work."

They had detected the thought and taken control before I had time to actuate it. Their minds simply made corrections that negated the thought before it allowed me to begin floating in the air.

"Forgive me," I said. "I did it without thinking. I have always wanted to fly on my own. There is still much to learn about this location."

The two of them laughed. Mirva said, "We have work to finish first."

"I understand," I replied, "and I like this teaching method better than that occurring during the meditation. This method doesn't affect my sleep."

Mataji nodded, and I understood that no reply was needed. "In this session," she said, "Mirva and I will take turns, one will give you instruction while the other assists in the demonstrations."

I nodded acceptance.

"Yesterday we promised to teach you more about the meditation called the Cosmic Whirlwind," she said. "Do you think you have its function completely mastered?"

"I know better than to say yes to that," I said.

"Why?"

"I learn something new about it almost every day," I said, "although you taught it to me long ago. In fact, it is one of the most important meditations I have learned."

"Are you aware of anything in particular that would make you think that?"

"Yes," I said. "The events of two nights ago."

"Can you tell us what gave you that opinion?"

"Yes," I said. "The many special things that happened to me during my near death experience. I have never read about anyone having an experience that paralleled my own."

"In what way?" She asked.

"Well, let's begin with a comparison of the similar. As the result of an accident or a severe illness, each of us had an out of body experience. Then we found ourselves floating in an area of space above our physical bodies, and surrounded by something resembling a tunnel of light. After a time of adjustment to what was happening, spiritual beings led us from earth toward a concentration of light at the end of a seemingly endless ascent through that passageway.

"In writing about their experiences, some tell us that for varying reasons they were told it was not their time to continue the experience. They were to return to their bodies and their life on earth experiences.

"Others tell of continuing through the tunnel, of varying experiences on that side of life, and then were told to return to earth and continue their former lives.

"All of them profited from the experience."

Both masters had shown intense interest in what I said. I knew they were aware of my thoughts, and felt they wanted me to put it into words. This would reinforce my understanding of this important matter. It was Mirva that told me to continue now with the differences.

"The main difference is the Masters' Meditation," I said. "You have taught me many meditation processes. Each one containing a powerhouse of experiences, each one filled with knowledge of the Universe and its immutable laws. Most of all, each one allowed me to touch into this Angelic Realm in some way, but always in the company of one of you Masters or Angels."

Mirva asked, "From what you have just said, what is your assessment of those earlier meditations?"

I had to think for a moment before I said, "Each one contains an important lesson, each one brings the student to a higher level of consciousness, each is a building block upon which the next one is founded. Yet each can stand alone in awakening within the meditator a powerful aspect of universal knowledge together with the ability to use it in perfecting earthly existence."

"What else?" She asked.

"When each of them is mastered in its proper order, and this includes the Cosmic Whirlwind, you come to the point where the Whirlwind also becomes an important tool. It can assist you in many additional ways."

"Tell us some of the ways."

"Whatever information you or Mataji gave me became important. She took me into the whirlwind meditation the first time I saw her."

It seemed strange for me to tell her about Mataji who sat quietly, listening to our conversation. During most of these sessions, both of their minds seemed to be fused as one while one of them spoke for both.

Mataji, of course, had heard my thought. She said, "Mirva and I are sisters. In our work with you, our every thought is unified in one and only one direction, that is to help you in every way we can in your work. We agreed to take this assignment, and you have agreed to work with us. The arrangement has been perfect."

We were in agreement. I said, "I have advanced to the level where I can instantly detect tension between others in my presence, no matter how much they try to hide it. When I am in the presence of masters, no tension is ever present. The powerful sensation of the Creator's unconditional love binds us together in that love, and I never want to be without it. Whenever I am in your presence, that sensation literally dances between you. It takes me in its arms at the same time and makes me part of that love.

"In the beginning of our study together, since I looked upon you as angels, I must confess that I felt a little guilty over the intensity of the love I felt for you. I was so young at that time, I didn't know the difference between God's love and that of the mundane. Very early in my career at sea, most of the passenger trade left the ships for the airlines, and my long ocean voyages found me surrounded by men of the staff that manned the ships.

## Chapter VIII

"There is an imbalance in the lives of those forced to live and work under those circumstances. It causes tensions and can lead to erratic behavior in all but those who are extremely well balanced.

"Since the two of you came to me in my meditations, that part of my life remained in balance. I used that balance to better understand the needs of others around me, and to create substitute programs that helped fill those needs. Your assistance helped me find ways to fill the need of others.

"Other masters came with you, to subtly touch the minds of the most needy and bring balance into their lives. The same spiritual love that flowed from my working with them, led me to understand that God's Eternal Presence manifested in every soul existing at your level.

"That brought me to a better understanding and an acceptance of the love existing between us. With it came the knowledge that everyone studying this meditation and working with their own masters, found their lives filled with Creation's Eternal Presence and everlasting joy.

"I have always known that joy and love in each and every instance of our personal contact. You came to me in person on a bitter cold morning in a lonely cabin in the Himalayas. The Eternal Presence accompanied you at that time. You told me of Mirva, and she came to me in meditation a year later. The same Presence also came with her. The two of you have been together in our meditations since that time. Each time you do, the energy is combined and enhanced. I have the best of both worlds and wish it would never end.."

"You were telling us the differences between your near death experience and that of others," Mataji said.

"The main difference," I said, "is the whirlwind. They discover the experience accidentally. They are blown along by the wind of spirit. Like debris drifting over the surface of an ocean, they have no control. You gave me the whirlwind. It is the tunnel leading from earth to eternity. In the Masters' Meditation, you taught me how to use it, and gave me a measure of control. From what the Archangel Rafael said two nights ago, I can now use it to bring the advanced meditators who study with me to this location. Will you show me how to do that?"

Mataji paused for a moment, "We never told you," she said. "How did you discover his name."

"Centuries ago," I said, "in another lifetime, long before you came into my life, he was my spiritual teacher when I was a healing monk in Inner Mongolia. Whenever you come into my presence, even though I may not see you, certain sensations flow within me, telling me you are here. I felt the same with him"

They both laughed. "We knew, of course," she said, "the moment it came into your mind."

I said. "Yet, long before that time, you have shown me incarnations where the three of us were together in lifetimes that found me at a higher level than I am in this."

I felt her sobering mood before she said, "We have felt your thoughts concerning this many times in the past. No one will tell you until the proper time. You know the reason we have not spoken of this, don't you."

"I volunteered to come, didn't I?"

"Yes," she said. "and that's enough for now. Let's get on with the teaching. I feel there is something else you want to tell us about the whirlwind. Tell us about it now."

## Chapter VIII

"In my advance class yesterday morning," I said, "as you know, we included some of the most powerful parts of the whirlwind. Everyone attending made exceedingly high level contact. When the class ended, they all wanted to tell of this special experience. When they finally left, you had already gone."

"We were with you, of course," they said. "Your new experiences allow you to advance at a more rapid pace. An increased energy accompanies each new level that you attain. The energy you transmit to the group takes each person into higher levels."

"Thanks," I said.

As I waited for what I knew would come, their minds merged in a display of dazzling energy that drew my mind into the vortex of the whirlwind surrounding their own. I closed my eyes as the rapture of the celestial contact expanded outward to accommodate the addition of two more angels—the same two that assisted us in the mental fusion that highlighted our first meeting at this level two nights ago.

As their minds became part of my own, a golden whirlwind surrounded us, its inner vortex slowly growing smaller as the wall of fire drew nearer. Standing in the center with their bodies surrounding me tightly, the spinning flame touched them first, filling them with the fiery energy.

As the radiant light infused them with unimaginable power, it moved inexorably through them. Their own fortified energy thrust inward into my own, lifting me ever higher, and sending my ever-increasing vibrations dancing up, down and around me, then mellowing into the super mind of Creation.

At that level we became a whirlwind. My own mind, no longer mine, became an expanded part of all of their minds, fusing my mind with that of Creation's own. A library of knowledge embracing the entire Cosmos, surrounded us and made us part of its own energy.

Four powerful angels had fused their own bodies into mine, their own minds into mine, and gave me the energy to elevate my own consciousness into total contact with this, Creation's own Consciousness. A superior mind that knew my wishes, my desires, my capabilities. It was a mind that would guide me through the final knowledge of the Cosmic Whirlwind and show me how it could help me finalize my earthly work.

A series of pictures began forming in my mind. As the first scene became clear, a man appeared in an isolated location, and the name Moses sounded within me. He fell upon the ground as a voice spoke to him from out of the fire within a whirlwind, a whirlwind similar to those I had used for years.

Other pictures: Mataji coming in her whirlwind during the night to a young shepherd boy. The name David merged in my mind, along with a picture of his using a slingshot to frighten the hungry wolves away from the lambs. Under Mataji's guidance, he continued to study the meditation. As he grew in wisdom, he followed his own path into enlightenment. History has recorded his contribution to the people of his world.

Another showed a picture of Elijah, embracing his own spiritual advancement, then creating his own whirlwind and allowing it to embrace him. His student, Elias, tells how the whirlwind carried Elijah bodily into heaven.

## Chapter VIII

These images depicted scenes from the past that I had remembered from my studies, with each one showing me how Creation's magic whirlwind worked in those special circumstances.

Now pictures of the unfamiliar danced one by one through my mind. each one showing men and women of importance, mentally creating and using the whirlwind in their lives.

From the inside, the golden whirlwind created a tunnel of light reaching into infinity. From the outside, it looked not at all unlike a tornado, encircled by a halo of golden radiance, extending from earth into the bluish golden cluster of light high above.

Out of the beautiful radiance of the Consciousness of Creation that surrounded our composite mind, came the sensation of Archangel Rafael's presence and the touch of his mind. My inner self recognized it from the past. A pleasant thought and a greeting surged through me from his mind, filling me with his special energy.

He had come to give me a glimpse of the future. His first picture showed me how the golden misty light of the Eternal Presence appeared to onlookers as it empowered the masters and angels with its embrace. His special energy attuned my vision, enabling me to more clearly see Creation's golden mist filling every aspect of space, every cubic meter, leaving no void.

Our special meditation told us of this golden mist from the beginning. My first book, Cosmic Fire, by virtue of its name announced God's Eternal Presence embracing and filling the mighty Cosmos.

We continue to study the Masters' Meditation. Each step we take along the Path, attunes us to the ever-increasing levels of vibration.  This enables us to more clearly see the golden mist of God's presence.  We see it everywhere.  It surrounds us completely.  Its energy flows into our bodies, fills us with energy, love, and belonging.

Our contact with and understanding of Creation's Laws grows stronger.  We now understand that this is the road to Everlasting Life   Our whirlwind becomes the tunnel from earth to Creation.  Our birthright, Everlasting Life, lies beyond the end of that tunnel.

The pictures continue.  I saw my introduction to the whirlwind by Mataji.  It was one among the many special meditations they taught me, its many special benefits had to wait until I learned the special techniques of those they taught me earlier.

Among the earlier studies, they taught me to construct a smaller personal whirlwind and use it in every aspect of my daily life.  I taught it to many of the earlier students, who used it successfully in their lives.  Its energy helped them, as well as me, to better focus our thoughts and attention on everything we had to do.  Success came more quickly and with less effort.

A music teacher learned how to construct and use the smaller personal whirlwind.  In his own teaching of music, he then began to teach his own students to think their own whirlwind into existence and place it around their own bodies while practicing.  The energy surrounding and filling their lives made learning easier and progress swifter.

I know of nothing else that can compare to the many wonders that flow to us so easily from this meditation.  The powerful mind of Rafael had shown me a few of the Whirlwind's most famous uses, once we are able to

## Chapter VIII

understand some of the things that it could accomplish.

Another picture showed me the familiar outline of the planet New Home. This planet had special meaning for many of the meditation students who worked with me. It is not generally known that the masters and angels gladly assist in the continuing process of Creation. They had used their creative powers and energy to bring that lifeless planet into full life-sustaining readiness.

While in meditation, our students follow the coming alive of this planet, knowing that its completion would enable them to go there in case such a need ever existed. In the process, they learned to love the planet itself and welcomed each new addition to its life-sustaining capacity.

Its nearness to our own solar system, when compared with the vastness of the cosmos, made it easily acceptable as a next door neighbor. They welcomed the fact that, as the nearest inhabitable planet, they wouldn't have a great distance to go should it ever become necessary.

Finally, the possibility that of such an idealistic mode of existence could be their own, opened them to accept it as their preferential home for the duration of eternity.

Rafael influenced me to see the planet New Home like a drop of water in an ocean, suggesting the existence of a limitless number of other possible habitats from which to choose. With so many other possibilities where life would be easier and more rewarding, why did so many of us cling to the limited pleasures of a dying earth? Why work so hard to gain so little, when the treasures of paradise could be attained with far less effort?

Pictures and instructions continued to flow from the mind of Rafael. In the future, the masters would help me take students to many of the other planets, similar to the New Home. In addition, we would visit other functioning planets, fully developed and inhabited.

Beyond that, with the assistance of my masters and guides, reliving the long and turbulent history of Creation became a possibility. From the sketches of information they showed me in the past, seeing it again in the clarity of this method, heightened my expectations.

The next chapter tells us more about the planet, New Home, and my two masters taking me on an introductory visit to that beautiful location.

## Chapter IX

### New Home

Another meditative visit to the angelic realm was now in progress. This time they used a different method of travel. Mirva's personal whirlwind moved swiftly through the intervening space between Planet Earth and the Planet New Home. Seated just behind her, Mirva and I were interested passengers. We looked past her shoulders as she mentally piloted her spacecraft to a soft landing on the virgin soil of the newly finished New Home planet.

A little larger than our own earth, its area could easily accommodate every living creature from our planet, and more. Other than variations in the size and configuration of the continents and oceans, it could easily have been a duplicate of planet earth—an earth untrammeled by the footsteps and occupation of our own species.

At our own masters' request, other masters of the Angelic Realm prepared the planet for our use, and had brought it to life; apparently filled with all species of life except mankind. Now it was ready for each of us who had found and was following this, the true path back to creation, under the guidance of the masters and angels.

Each one of us who has earned the privilege to exist at a higher level of consciousness can seek residency at the end of their present incarnation, or when and if it should become necessary before that time.

While similar to planet earth, as are most of the other planets in Creation, the history of New Home is unique. In preparation for our use, it had been reconstructed into an exact duplicate of one of the earlier inhabited planets that had to be sacrificed to make room for an ever-expanding universe.

Its inhabitants had reached a higher level of consciousness than we have attained. Their way of life paralleled that which we might look to find in the promised Eden of existence we call Heaven. Reluctant to leave paradise, they agreed to live on another similar planet located in a different part of the Cosmos.

Many of their race had already attained the level of ascended master, and earned the privilege of a parallel existence on their own planet. They continued to live in the paradise of their own native planet, which they called Home, until the time came for them to leave.

What might have been considered an anomaly in the angelic realm, spacecraft transported them en masse to a new planet already prepared for them in another galaxy. They never forgot their original home, and carried the sacred memory of that existence in their hearts.

They took the same style of life with them to the new planet, with very little change except location. Life went on as before the change of location, amid peace, plenty, and the joy of existing in the beloved Eternal Presence.

News of the reconstruction of the planet to be called New Home spread through the many habitable universes. Since leaving their Old Home, these advanced souls had spread out, forming enchanting settlements of their own in many parts of the Cosmos. Some resolved to resettle on New Home when it was completed.

Prior to leaving their old home, the masters from that mighty race had found an uninhabitable planet and quietly given it the name New Home. Using the special powers they had attained as masters, they created a museum within that planet. It consisted of a long, well lit corridor leading deep within, with doors leading from the corridor

## Chapter IX

into many rooms located on each side.

Each of these rooms contained replicas of a special part of life as they had known it. It contained a separate room for each activity of the people. For instance, a series of rooms dedicated to the arts, another group dedicated to its music, another to its sciences. It continued with room after room of exhibits until every aspect of life and existence on that planet was displayed and made available for all to see and enjoy whenever they wished

As part of my continuing education, Mataji and Mirva had carried me meditatively to New home during the many years of our association. I understand it now as part of their project to teach me the real truth about Creation and our own relationship to the Cosmos.

The instruction began in the dream like world of the Masters' Meditation. Countless learning sessions followed in this and other learning centers existing in the mighty Cosmos, of which we are but a tiny part. With our minds so closely linked, I could see plans for future visits to some of those other locations where part of the history of earth and that of Creation can be examined and revealed.

We spent many happy days in the museums of New Home. Under the direction of these two powerful masters, we meditatively shared the idyllic existence of the dwellers and the joy that filled their lives.

My teachers guided my mind along that beautiful path. They opened their minds and allowed me to share their own sensations as they shared with the inhabitants the joy of living under the protective love of what they called The Eternal Presence. It filled their lives and every aspect of life on the planet.

They reminded me of the first time they took me back in meditation to visit the Old Home planet as it existed near the beginning of time. We lived among the people, and shared their lives and their pleasures with them as it was in the early years after Creation.

These were the first people. Created in the image of the angels, they shared many of the angels' talents, but with human forms much less dense than the bodies we now possess. In other words, they could either fly through the air or walk on their earth, determined only by the set of their minds.

My strongest memory is the quality of life that existed among these people. The Eternal Presence filled every moment of time with the pure love of the Creator. The security of that relationship provided the minor miracles they performed like magic in even the simplest task their hands found to do.

Like the masters and angels that have been part of my life for so long, the powers of their minds produced their every need. With them, greed was unknown. Without it, no police force existed. Each worked for the common good of all. Perfection and the quality of life prevailed.

Yet, the birthright of every person on our earth allows them through free choice to seek and find a way back to this paradise we lost a long time in the past. I have found this way in this beautiful meditation. The choice, as always, is yours. I can only show you the way.

My teachers continued the instructions by helping me understand that bringing a barren planet to life is not a difficult task for the masters. The most difficult from our own point of view would be the element of time, but for them they have no problem with that element.

## Chapter IX

We have casually considered this topic before. It has now become important to understand it in detail When we think of time, we see the hands of the clock moving slowly around the face of the timepiece. Compare the passage of time from our point of view to that of those dwelling at the level of everlasting life, which is the abode of the masters and angels. Time at that level considers only the everlasting life. There is no past, and no future—only that of the eternal present.

Many people share the Masters' Meditation and its beautiful experience with me. Afterwards, when I tell them the length of time we were in meditation, the most frequent response is, "It seemed like it was only a few minutes."

Consider the importance of the above statement. In the meditation, we move in spirit from earthly time, which moves forward in a straight line, to the eternal present where time exists only in the eternal now. One of the most important results is this: in meditation, the body is keeping earth's time, while the mind and spirit are in the eternal now, where time is non-existent.

That will explain the little-known statement that we mentioned above, and much more. It also allows me to disclose for the first time an important element of the meditation not easily understood. When the sincere students of this meditation completely masters the process and begins to study under his or her own masters, they can make good use of the difference in times for long periods of exploring or learning on the spiritual plane, in a seemingly short period of earthly time.

Think of that time factor when you recall my visits to the museums of New Home. Imagine the unlimited joy that was mine, while surrounded by my masters, and relaxed in a recliner in a private box at their Opera House.

Remember that this performance reflected all of the culture of Old Home. You not only saw and heard, but lived and experienced every emotion they presented. Virtual reality came into being at the Old Home, almost at the beginning of time. That and much more. Every new thing that we experienced carried with it the same degree of perfection.

My angelic masters continued to teach me new and powerful truths about this, which would be the other side of an existence, one that was opposite from their own. The pictures from the minds of my teachers continued to flow into my own. They showed that almost from the beginning of earth time, myth had perpetuated stories of creation and its powerful spiritual beings that were at variance with that which I had been shown for almost half a century.

The Masters' Teachings had never varied from the beginning. Their language had always been pictures and symbols. My mind created words for those pictures, and I always understood in my own language.

Since my near death experience, my time with these teachers had become much clearer and more realistic. Even in the peaceful contact with the Eternal Presence, a sense or urgency manifested strongly in their pictures and in their attitude. It was just there. I knew it, and I knew they understood. When I asked them why, they always said everything was proceeding on schedule. Other than that, we continued as before.

From the thousands of rooms and exhibits scattered within the interior of New Home, we could sample every

## Chapter IX

facet of existence that made the original Home such a delightful place to live or visit. I liked to come here with my teachers. They seemed to know everything about it, and the light of love shone from their eyes as they lovingly explained each priceless detail.

Many of the masters from the old Home who took part in the construction of this museum earlier, had helped to bring the outer surface back to life. They now worked in the museum, happily teaching others who had come to learn from these masters while waiting for the official opening of the planet for settlement. There would be more than enough space for everyone.

I easily shared the love my masters felt for the New Home. They brought me here so often, it became as familiar to me as my own home. I waited for them to tell me more since I felt that Erna and I had shared a lifetime at the old Home. I often saw visions of her as a young girl, happily playing with other children in the spacious out of doors of that beautiful planet. She is my wife now, and that fact clouds my understanding. But I would happily have had her as my daughter or sister should that have been true at that time.

The unconditional love of the Eternal Presence shines brightly upon those who have earned acceptance at that level. Love, as we know and identify it in our own world, has its place in our life, but it has never satisfied all of our needs. If it had, we would have peace upon earth. The love found in the Eternal Presence at the higher levels fills every need for those who have earned the right to live under its blanket of personal protection joined together with the fullness of its everlasting life and love.

For reasons known only to the Creator, souls from the

angelic realm volunteer for one or more lifetimes on earth. It is a learning experience on that special planet, where the body takes on a temporary materialistic density and one has the free will to exist outside the mantel of the Eternal Presence. For me, life under those conditions is a painful and meaningless experience.

Those who have hope and believe there is a better way, join me on the path back to Creation. They can do that through personal classes with me, or through the medium of my home study meditations. They learn to come to this or other areas of the angelic realm, and experience the pleasures of that location for themselves.

A thought came to me from the minds of my teachers. "You are almost ready to begin that teaching," they said. "In only a few more days, we will begin."

"I am ready," I replied.

## Chapter X

### The Real Truth

We had returned to the opera house and resumed our seats in our own special box. Following the mental direction of my masters, my eyes closed automatically. My teachers understood the meaning of the silent messages playing delightfully within my psyche, and interpreted them for me.

My angelic masters, committed to teaching me every facet of the unlimited reach of their own meditation, revealed for the first time that it originated from within the perfection of the Eternal Presence. The lessons they taught with their minds materialized easily into my own. It existed everywhere, as part of the misty glow surrounding each of us, as part of the Eternal Presence that filled us with Its love.

I still relaxed on my recliner, with sounds of exotic music playing gently upon each of my enraptured senses. The same rapture filled my consciousness. It also flowed from the minds of my teachers, and mingled with my own as my enlightenment continued.

"You seemed surprised," Mataji said, "when we told you where our meditation originated. Your thinking had led us to assume you already knew."

I said, "I accepted it as truth long ago. My heart knew there could be no other answer. In something of this major importance, its comforting to know the truth."

"We saw that conviction in your mind," she said. "Are you aware of any limits?"

"From what I have learned, I can neither think of nor foresee any limits."

"There are none," she confirmed.

The misty golden light of the Eternal Presence that surrounded us, rose to higher levels of radiance. The blanket of love of that Presence, that held me snugly in its arms, tightened gently around me  They allowed me to float in that ocean of love for what could have been an eternity. Roving fingers of the golden radiance touched special locations within me, gently massaging them into a perfection found only at this level.

They knew I needed time and opportunity to adjust to the final confirmation of what I had long ago suspected. These three simple words Mataji had just mentioned would change my life forever. There are none, she had said. The astonishing significance of those words flowed through my mind with the speed of a supersonic jet. It dazzled my senses to consider the effect this knowledge would have on the people of our planet.

Here, in the expanded consciousness found only in the angelic realm, the full importance of that revelation raced outward in every direction. Having mastered this meditation, I could come into these higher levels with my masters whenever I wished. Only one problem remained, how could I possibly bring it to the attention of so many others who needed to know these truths so desperately.

A series of pictures trailed swiftly across my mind. I saw our entire planet shrouded in a dark blanket of misinformation. With almost everyone pressuring us into accepting their unsupported beliefs, finding the simple truth would be difficult, almost impossible. If each person who found this truth would only pass it on to someone else, we might have a chance. We could hope they would tell others, but that is not the way things happened.

The pictures came to me from the minds of my angelic

## Chapter X

teachers. Their experience with earth's frailties were of a longer duration than the half century they had worked with me. Despite the many disappointments of the past, they tirelessly supported my efforts to once again bring their meditation to the world.

Mataji's mental confirmation, There are none, spoke volumes. It said that this meditation carries within it limitless possibilities for personal development. Step by step, through a magnificent series of ever-expanding meditations, the path back to the beginning is revealed.

That beautiful road back to the Eternal Presence has always existed, even from the beginning of time. Not a road where you took upon your back the burden of the world's problems, and trudged aimlessly with the masses in a wilderness of obstacles with no end in sight. Once you find the Masters' Meditation, you leave behind those burdens. Then from each joyful meditation, you walk hand in hand with spiritual guides and angelic masters. You are always under their gentle guidance and protection while on the spiritual plane. With your safety thus assured, you can relax and allow them to take you into the joyous rapture that is their own meditation.

Confirmation of the divine origin of this meditation came to me again and again over the years that I used it and taught it to others. My first book, Cosmic Fire, told of those early teaching years. Many people studied with me, enjoying the unexpected energy and the many benefits originating within those introductory processes.

Most of them had families and their work occupied nearly all of their waking hours. Through it all, they only had little time left for meditation. They utilized those spare minutes wisely after the meditations became part of their lives.

With practice, they quickly mastered those beginning taped meditations. After that, they entered into the altered state whenever they found a free moment of time. In just a few minutes, they returned to their work completely refreshed and at peace with the world. Cross country truck drivers who use this method, report that with only ten minutes of such meditation in a rest area, they resumed driving with the same feeling as that mentioned above.. Completely relaxed, they drove more safely and with less stress.

From the above, it is easy to see how the Masters' Meditation fills an important need in the lives of almost everyone in our busy Western World.

Pictures from the minds of my teachers continued to move slowly through my mind. They showed me an endless line of our students whom I had never met in person but, over the past 15 years, had begun this meditative study through our home study service.

I correspond with many of these students, especially when they begin to master the early lessons and its many benefits begin to manifest in their lives. The first session is powerful, and for most of them rewards begin with this first meditation.

Those first lessons serve them well. The ecstasy felt at the beginning is so powerful, many remain at that level. With such powerful results, some think that is all there is to the meditation, and are content to repeat it for the remainder of their lives.

I often receive a request a few years later, for another set of the beginning tapes. Although the continuity was discussed in the beginning, many had forgotten. They

## Chapter X

found such satisfaction with the first tapes, in their busy lives, they enjoyed what they had and never thought beyond that point.

Happy to learn that there were additional tapes, they were eager to continue with the course. In the easy beginning meditation, I found that they hadn't even read the manual of instruction. Even without instructions, the tapes satisfied their needs.

The mental pictures continued to flow. I wondered why my teachers showed me pictures from the past that I knew so well, but I had learned never to ask questions. In due time a very good reason for these reminders would come to me, usually at the exact time I had learned how to properly use it.

Scenes from the advanced classes now appeared. Many of this group smiled to me, as the pictures came alive in my mind. Just when I believed myself to have reached the highest possible level of contact, the Eternal Presence grew stronger as I remembered the many beautiful meditations I had shared with some of them that I taught in person.

Mataji said, "We guided you through those contacts. We remember them with pleasure also."

"Thank you for the memories," I said. "I know there is a reason, and I am afraid to even ask."

"There is nothing for you to be afraid of," she said. "The same is true for most of those we have just shown you. We can see in your mind that you understand why."

"At the higher levels of consciousness we are now working in," I said, "without your guidance and love, the evil and hatred that flows free over our planet would be unbearable."

"That's why we refreshed your memory," she said. "You have accomplished more than you think. Those who smiled at you are well on their way to full contact with the Eternal Presence. You will soon be showing them the New Home planet, and taking them for visits to the angelic realm.

"We will be with you each time you take them into these higher levels. You have been with us for such a long time, we need your voice to help bring them to these levels. In time, they will have the same rapport with their own masters as you have with us. Then they can explore the Cosmos with their masters, as you have been doing with us for so long."

I thought for a moment before speaking. "Can you tell me how much time we have left?" I asked.

"No one knows for sure," she said. "It has been written that not even the angels know the day or the hour. That is almost true, for we do know the disasters are coming with more frequency and greater severity. It is only a matter of time.

"This mission offers you the greatest hope for earth's survival. If it fails, it offers you its greatest hope for those who have found this bridge to eternity.

"You have had the benefit of an intimate association with masters and angels for many years. Remember, your first guide, Joshua, contacted you as a child. He guided you throughout almost all your life before we came to you as a young man. That made it easy for you to see how easy it was to work with angels if you tried and really believed. We will continue to work with you, and help you as you pass on to others what you have learned.

"We have concentrated much of the information and

meditative technique we gave you in less than a dozen special meditations. You have recorded them under our direction. We will assist you in getting the tapes into the hands of all who are searching for the truth. Every master and angel in this realm will assist each person who asks. And we will consider each person who reaches out for that help as having asked."

My mind sensed the force of the powerful mind of Mirva echoing strongly behind each thought coming to me from the angel Mataji. The combined force burned into my mind in fiery letters of the golden light of Creation. Never before had I ever seen myself as anything other than one of the great mass of humanity, struggling for survival, searching for the light.

She always knew my thoughts. "There is one great difference," Mataji said, "you agreed to do this before you were born."

"I have always assumed that I agreed beforehand," I said. "Thank you for the confirmation."

The gentle vibrations of light and love of the Eternal Presence that held me warmly, tightened Its embrace just a little in reassurance. At this level, my expanded mind, in tune with the perfection of the universe, counted one by one each simple universal Vibration that made its function an element of God's Perfection.

Even Einstein saw the lowest Vibrations as varying manifestations of matter, and the highest Vibrations as manifestations of Light. In his struggles to present these laws of Vibrations in an equation the world could use and understand, he did not take into consideration the fact that only those who had attained the Eternal Presence could fully understand and use that knowledge.

In his ego, mankind immediately made this knowledge into a terrible weapon of destruction long before it had been perfected for peaceful use. Concerned only with maintaining dominance over others, they lost sight of their arrogant misuse of God's energy, thus setting in motion the instrument of their own destruction.

These and other pictures continued to flow through my mind. Everything that is was created by God. The soul had its origin in God and always remained as a part of that Origin. The human body was created from the lower vibrations of earth.

When the mind turns its thoughts into the direction of the light, and finds the perfection of the Eternal Presence, the lower vibrations of the body become redefined and purified. Continued use of the Masters' Meditation, will enhance the progress, thus lifting the body into higher levels of being, and the soul into higher level of spiritual consciousness.

The connection is then perfect. We will have reached a state of perfect equilibrium. Our guides then allow us to see the entire universe, most of it consisting of worlds of the angelic realm that are already ripe with harvest, ready and waiting for those who have eyes to see to grow up and claim their birthright.

It is up to us. The Masters' Meditation is the only way I have ever found to reach that level, The pictures that come to me also show the hate, murder, war and rebellion in our own world. If you are disturbed by scenes of innocent people blown away by bombs and guns, and know that you could also become a victim, you can join us on this beautiful path back to the Creator with the little time that remains. It might just possibly save your life.

## Chapter XI

### Tschen Li and Karma

An almost undetectable sense of urgency attended each teaching session. My two teachers called me almost every night with an agenda filled with new and different subjects to cover. I had learned from experience that when two powerful masters gave almost all of their precious time to one individual, I should give them my total attention and not ask questions. As usual, they sensed my thoughts. In their wisdom, at some point in each session they included a reassuring picture and a thought that told me all was proceeding as planned.

They had summoned me from a deep sleep. For an unusual length of time we ascended without the usual myriad of lights dancing past us. Then, like fireflies on a summer evening, flickering dots of multicolored lights surrounded us, increasing in number and slowly growing brighter.

Mataji and Mirva stood at my sides, the warmth of their hands on my arms giving me the reassurance of their presence. We entered the Angelic Realm amid soothing patterns of glowing lights announcing our arrival.

Embraced in the golden mist of the Eternal Presence, we floated gently into our special chamber where the angel Raphael, with two of his angelic assistants, waited. They greeted us warmly as they moved closer, and quietly formed a circle around us.

A familiar whirlwind took form in the golden mist, surrounding us with its radiance. Vibrations of light intensified as the whirling motion encased us in a circle of fire. The bodies of the angels pressed closely upon mine. The energy of the whirlwind, already flowing into their own bodies, passed into mine, intensifying the volume of energy within me. In the total fusion of our souls and minds that came into being in an instant, the composite mind of the angels lifted my own into total contact with the highest level of consciousness.

The powerful mind of the archangel Raphael gently touched mine. He said, "We have now connected your mind with that of Creation. Take time to see the immensity of the Cosmos. You saw much of it once before. Examine it again in more detail. Tell of its existence in your writing. The only way to reach it from your level is through our meditation."

Pictures of the mighty Cosmos from the Divine Mind had already begun flowing into my awareness. I said. "I can see the pictures now."

"We have given you the connection," he said. "It will remain in place as long as your two guides wish. This session is important. You have a lot to learn. I wish you well in your studies."

While in meditation, Mataji and Mirva had shown me many of these locations in the past. The death experience of a few days ago had carried me into the same locations with a near perfect clarity, a clarity that continued to occur in each subsequent session with my teachers.

Rafael must have signed off for Mataji continued with the instructions. Her thoughts came clearly, even as pictures of other worlds and livable planets flowed in my mind. She said, "You have reached a level where the improved spiritual contact is now permanent. You must have known that continued meditation always brings continued growth."

When we began the study almost 50 years ago, the

newness, the unusual nature of this powerful meditation, filled me with its gentle peace. It brought joy and love to my soul that was filled with sadness from participating in a cruel war where so many lives were needlessly destroyed.

The guns of war became silent. The guides told me the silence was only temporary. The guns would come alive again and again. The final peace would not come until man put away his greed, turned from his conflict, and sought the peace of the angels that existed in a dimension only a few steps separate from their own.

When they told me it could be found in the present lifetime in this simple meditation, it gripped me with a passion and a resolution. They told of a world where the Eternal Presence of our benevolent Creator hovered like a safety blanket and held us in its arms of Everlasting love. A world of love where every soul existed in love and safety that intensified that passion and led to the resolution to work with these two masters as long as they were willing to assist.

They said that those who joined me in the serious study of the Masters' Meditation, would find the sullen density of their physical bodies continuing to grow lighter. Their light bodies of the soul and mind would dance with a joy found only in the spiritual contact with masters and angels. The final reward would be attaining mastery of life and the ability to step easily into that higher dimension. Then they could remain at that level forever.

Their work consisted of bringing this powerful method into the lives of as many of us as they could reach. But we had to go to them. I had answered their call, learned their teaching and taught it to others. No easy task in our overworked world that is submerged in greed. In looking to others for salvation, we are looking in the wrong direction. For our salvation is within each of us. We need only to look within. Once you do, you will find that our simple meditation will carry us all the way.

In my long association with the masters, I had seen that happen only once. My beloved Tibetan master and teacher, Tschen Li, easily took that step into everlasting life after working with me for 32 years. He introduced me to the wonders of this meditation and taught me for the first year. After that, the masters Mataji and Mirva joined in the teaching and taught me from the exalted world of the angels. Other masters eventually joined the group and assisted from the same high level.

Tschen Li continued to personally work with me on the earthly plane. From the beginning, I saw him exhibit unusual talents that exceeded that of any other human. He would sometimes rise slowly into the air while we both were in meditation. He would often disappear for short periods of time during our meditative sessions, while the telepathic instructions continued to flow evenly in my mind during his absence.

He demonstrated teleportation by traveling great distances in an instant. He manifested anything he needed using only the powers of his mind. He spoke many languages with ease, a difficult task for all but those in tune with Universal Knowledge. His demeanor was that of an humble man. He never carried cash, but manifested only what he needed. He had attained complete mastery of life, yet did nothing for show or personal gain.

The amazing talents demonstrated by Tscen Li are important He practiced this meditation from age 12, and credited it for his attaining a long and fruitful lifetime. He

## Chapter XI

used the special abilities possessed only by masters and angels during the 32 years that he was my earthly teacher. He made the ascension to the angelic realm at a time when he considered his life's work on earth finished.

Many of the people who have studied with me now possess differing levels of this meditation. The masters have told me that I have advanced to the level where, like Tschen Li, I can teach it to those students and others as my teachers gave it to me. Therefore, everyone who has studied with me, who are studying with me now or begin to study in the future, can look forward to the possibility of attaining these abilities and eventual ascension to the much desired angelic realm.

In my opinion, no matter how long it requires, there is nothing on earth more important than attaining that goal.

Mataji changed the direction of my visions. I now stand on a distant planet, my soul and mind merged with five powerful angels, my own mind elevated into contact with the Infinite Mind of the Universe, they allow me to see anything I wish to see, all the way to the end of an eternity, which has no end.

They have shown me thousands of habitable planets that are ready for humanity to come and enjoy. I see fertile land, gentle soothing rain that comes at regular intervals, where life is pleasant and there is no conflict.

I am almost ready to make my transition from earth to the angelic realm, which is composed of all of Creation except our own earth. I have elected to remain and teach their Masters' Meditation as long as they wish. A decision that keeps my physical body chained to the frailties of life here on earth, while my mind and consciousness view what some might call the promised land.

From this level where my mind is linked to that of the Infinite Mind, it is easy to see planet earth with their eyes. Mataji told me later that at this time, what they did not show me was my physical body, sitting in a trance in my study back on earth, and recording these thoughts and pictures into my computer. The connection between us is perfect, and these observations come entirely from the Divine Mind.

The probable future of earth is not good. To begin with, the solid surface of the crust is unstable and has no cohesion. It is filled with cracks that form hundreds of tectonic plates scattered over its surface. Its instability increases with the increased inner pressure and the frequency and force of its volcanoes and earthquakes. Surface patterns of the weather make frequent changes that make life difficult and uncertain. It is evident that earth was settled too soon. It required more time to mature and become stable.

That uncertainty and the fear it brings with it, causes many of our problems. We see it all around us. Life can be snuffed out at any moment; disasters, wars and conflict happen without notice. Most of us live only for the now and search for some form of security. Hence the greed, the hoarding, reaching in every direction for the imagined security of more items of material possessions than we need. There is never enough.

Fear and uncertainty continue to heighten as new viral infections appear. They spread rapidly. Science has found neither cure nor prevention. Angered and fearful men have formed armed gangs, ostensibly for their own safety, but their very existence adds only fuel to the flame of total imminent destruction.

## Chapter XI

At the height of this special session, with my mind in tune with that of the angels to the wisdom and knowledge of the universe, these fearful visions give me the angel's view of how they perceive conditions on earth at this time. I sense their great sorrow as their sensitive minds cringe when they feel all of the negative emotions flowing from planet earth pounding the surface of the dimensional barrier between us as we struggle vainly to escape.

When the masters allow the simple solution to these problems to flow into my own mind, I find that I knew the answer all along. A simple meditation, entrusted to me by special masters. It came to me a long time ago, when I had just reached the height of my career, and my increased earnings provided a surplus that could be applied to the debt incurred by my education. My scientific schooling almost prevented me from accepting the masters' gift when it was first offered. Fortunately Tschen Li looked within and found the real me. A man of many talents, he easily convinced me to agree.

That incident happened on the second day he came into my life. They permitted me to continue my work, to get my affairs in order, and to cruise blissfully through a great adventure at the same time. The adventure of studying with teachers from the angelic realm, helped me learn their laws and philosophy, and apply those principles to my own life. At the same time, with my mind attuned intimately with theirs, I found pleasure in each of the many special meditative sessions we shared.

Although I concur with the thoughts these writings bring to your mind, these thoughts emerge from the minds of angelic masters and angels. It is their direction that I put these thoughts on paper for the ultimate guidance of everyone on earth.

These spiritual beings, with their minds as part of the mind of God, could mentally force any change they desired upon the people of planet earth. Yet they are bound by a Divine Decree of the Creator that gives people free will to live life as they desire. In so doing, they have to accept the responsibility of their actions.

The masters call it the Law of consequence. Some Eastern cultures refer to it as Karma. By whatever name it is called, the end result is always the same. The biblical expression, "As you sow, so shall you reap." says it simpler and by implication more forcibly.

## Chapter XII

### An Angel's View of Planet Earth

The accelerated pattern of teaching continued on a nightly basis. After about three hours of deep sleep each night, it seemed that with my teachers, almost anything could happen. Tonight was no exception.

The summons came at its usual time. Each ascension took a different pattern. In only seconds, the thrilling vibrations of ascending through space embraced me. The familiar continents and oceans of the planet New Home flashed briefly in my vision. An instant later, the luxury of soft cushions welcomed me to my own lounging chair in what passed for them as their opera house.

Still half asleep, the sensory impressions of multi-dimensional music welcomed my arrival by holding me in its gentle embrace. A soothing awareness reaching deep within filled me with its unique rapture.

The Eternal Presence of the Creator reached out and included me in Its special protection. I simply moved into Its gentle presence which, as always, surrounded Mataji and Mirva. They welcomed me from their usual chairs, located on either side of my own.

Both of their minds, already bound into a single unit, reached out and embraced that of my own. My mind followed theirs into an intense focus on the mental pictures already beginning to flow through my awareness,

The composite scene depicted a typical day on earth. They had placed me in the center of awareness of the millions of events happening simultaneously in selected locations all over the planet.

My total awareness mingled closely with that of their own. My expanded mind vividly pictured the pages out of our own human drama they wanted me to see.

A tidal wave of negative horror struck me from every side at the same instant. I struggled in vain to close my eyes, to look away, to see something else. Wherever they turned my reluctant vision, similar scenes filled every atom of the space surrounding us.

They forced me to look directly into the face of the utter terror of human beings lashing out against each other with an array of unbelievable weapons of hate, inhuman actions and utter destruction.

Accustomed to seeking only the good I had found and worked with for a lifetime, I could find none of that good evident in the scenes they now put before me. It was in there somewhere I knew, but totally outnumbered, it lay buried in the chaotic wave of agony.

As I watched the varying patterns of the pictures flowing through my mind, I knew their presentations were only a general representation of life on earth and how it had become a world apparently gone mad, despite the existence of various movements for peace.

Welcomed instructions from their mind came to me at the correct time. They said, "The energy created by the wild frenzy of madness overcomes the peaceful energy of those working for the overall good."

"I know," I said. "The various news media have found that the conflict within bad news sells better than the lack of it in good news. It attracts more listeners. For them, it is the matter of money. Their monetary profits are greater. And that's the bottom line, as anyone in business will tell you.."

"What is the answer?" They asked.

"I must work more effectively." I said. "What can I

do to get the message to more of the people seeking only the good?"

"Look deeply within our minds." They suggested.

The answer reached out to me from the sparkling radiance of their minds. "First, they must learn our meditation. There they can experience the supreme joy of walking in the Eternal Presence of the Creator. Once they experience that joy and ecstasy, and the great Love of God that goes with it, they will know that nothing on earth can ever satisfy again. We, of course, will continue to help as we have in the past."

"Can you tell me how to reach those minds?" I asked.

Total attunement to the minds of these two angelic guides, brought me back into the great love of the Creator's Eternal Presence. The sadness that surrounded me moments before, gave way to a joyous reunion with that love and the supreme ecstasy of sharing it with the angels.

In the light of that love came the answer from their minds. "The answer lies within what we call our own meditation, but it is not our own as its name implies. We are only the custodians, the messengers carrying the joyful news of its existence and offering it freely to everyone."

"Then give me the words to adequately describe what we have to offer," I said. "How do I describe a joy and a love so wonderful, the highest earthly pleasure pales in comparison?"

"You did well with that sentence. Try to think of hundreds more just like it."

"Then tell me how to describe that which seems impossible to put into words. I am thinking of things like the healing energy of creation flowing through every part of the body, and feeling minor pains slowly diminishing and then disappearing. Knowing you are entering into a period of improving health. Sensing the energy of youth returning, and with it the physical joy of feeling good again. Most of all, finding the road back to Creation, and following it into ever-increasing spiritual contact.

"It is like floating in a sacred ocean of love. You know that it can only come from the mind and heart of God. You become immersed in the energy of that Love. Your own personal family who have gone on before you, are with you in the physical part of existence, and as your companions and guides, make that part of your life easier and more rewarding.

"You are in constant contact with the Divine Mind of the Creator. That knowledge is available for you to use in every aspect of your daily existence, It gives you perfect understanding of the natural laws or rules of the universe, and of your own personal relationship to every little part of the mighty Cosmos.

"Your live in perfect balance with all of that wisdom and love. You still have free will. You can do what you choose. But contact with the All enables you to know in an instant the consequence of any action that you might make on your own. You know that you will never do anything to diminish the perfection of life when it is lived in the joy and Love of the Eternal Presence of God."

They said, "You have summed it up nicely, but keep trying and you will learn to do it even better."

They wanted me to keep on writing, and trying to put the rapture of these precious moments into adequate terms of human communion. Of course I will continue to write words that try to describe the depth of my feelings.

## Chapter XII

Yet I know of no vocabulary or language capable of putting such feelings into words.

The beginning meditations are beautiful, filled with joy and ever-increasing ecstasy that increases progressively as the student continues. Everyone continues to increase their ever upward.movement. There is no limit to the ultimate possibility of advancement.

The two masters at my side are really angels, I thought to no one in particular. They are messengers of God.. They had attained the highest possible level of existence, the ability to reside in the angelic realm with all of its wonders and benefits. Its perfection would endure forever.

I knew that on earth there was nothing of value to us at that level that could be of interest to them. For they have it all. With their minds and consciousness permanently attuned to vibrations of the angelic realm, and with the essence of their being existing in the glory of Creation for Eternity, they are in total contact with the Creative Mind of the Universe, which is the Creator, or God, or whatever name mankind in its ignorance may have used to identify It.

It makes no difference. They are permanent residents of that Realm, and are a part of Its Creative structure. In that capacity, in their contact with the Creative Mind, they are part of that Mind. They are possessors of an asset of immense value. Nothing in all of the mighty Cosmos could possibly compare.

Neither the possessions of kings, emperor, nor the richest person who ever existed, could ever have anything that approached the value of one special asset possessed by the two angelic masters now reclining in easy chairs, one on either side of my own.

With their minds as part of the Creative Mind of the Universe, they have the power to create anything they wish with their minds by mentally picturing it as already existing in any location they desired.

Yet, in their total contact with the Eternal Presence, they were always wrapped in the mantle of that great Love. The pleasure, the joy and bliss of living in that Great Presence, exceeded that of any of earth's feeble pleasures. It satisfied every desire.

In that environment, despite the ability to mentally create anything they wished, the masters manifested only enough to fill their needs. Having touched into that level, I knew the reason. The joy of living at that level exceeded any of earth's pleasures or satisfactions.

They have often told me that material possessions are a hindrance to their mobility. Why should they tediously lug bulky possessions behind them, when they can create anything they need upon arrival at their new location?

In considering the life patterns of the masters, another thought came naturally to me. Throughout my many years of association with them, never once did the thought of remuneration cross my mind.

In return, they gave me the gift of the precious Masters' Mediation with all of its many benefits. In my spare time, they taught me the foundation of philosophical knowledge which supported their teachings.

In recent days they revealed that this special meditation came into existence as part of the first force of Creation as that great burst of energy surged across the Universe. As part of a small group of angelic masters, my own teachers had custody of the process, and the obligation to take it to the world, to anyone who could and would use it to attain the same benefits.

The awesome impact of that revelation surges through me with that same initial force, each time remembrance of their words touches my mind.

My first meditation teacher, Tschen Li, had the same special abilities possessed by the masters. He did not reveal that to me in the beginning. Like all other monks, his earthly appearance was no different, and there was nothing to suggest his special abilities. But as our relationship continued, and my expanding consciousness moved upward swiftly under his guidance, I saw little departures out of the ordinary that revealed a special talent.

His trust in my discretion came quickly. He soon began teaching me how to use this ability myself when I reached a certain level of wisdom and understanding. I did not have his advantage of beginning the study of the Eastern meditation at age six, or that of having Mataji come in spirit at age twelve and begin teaching the Masters' Meditation at that time.

With all of those benefits, he began developing these powers soon after he passed the century mark. I am happy to wait until these benefits come to me at the proper time in my spiritual development. It's a comfort to know that I will have them when I have earned the right to cross the Bridge to Eternity for the last time and become one with them at that level.

Think for a moment of this one final benefit to those who seriously study and learn this meditation. Every sincere student has the same opportunity that I have, or that which Tschen Li possessed, or the many others down through history who found this special road back to Creation, and earned the right to follow it to its ultimate reward.

Even from the first meditation, each step that you take is one of supreme joy. The golden light of the Creator shines brightly above you, His great love wraps you in Its blissful arms, you walk in the Eternal Presence of the Creator forever. Nothing else in Creation can even remotely compare to this final meditative benefit.

My two teachers remained relaxed in deep thought in the comfort of their recliners. When they made no effort to send me back, I knew they had more to show me. It will be covered in the next chapter.

## Chapter XIII

### Free will and Karma.

Total attunement to the minds of these two angelic masters was its own reward. The ultimate benefit of our association came in moments like this, when they took me by the hand and led me across that sacred bridge, and gave me the honor of sharing with them a few moments in this, the angelic realm. Some call it eternity or everlasting life.

They brought me in spirit to this and other locations within this high level on a nightly basis. It was part of the masters' plan to bring awareness of their wonderful meditation to as many of earth's people as possible, and to show them the rewards coming to those who made it part of their lives.

To return to the physical for a moment, my wife just opened the door to my computer room and asked in a soft voice when would I come back to bed. It aroused me from total contact with the minds of the masters and I remember that my voice said, "Soon." A moment later I found myself back on the planet New Home, relaxing in my own recliner, and in total contact with Mataji and Mirva.

The merged minds of my two masters reached out and touched mine. They asked, "Since we have given you enough material for another chapter, you think you know the reason for this special meeting."

"I sensed an overall meaning," I said, "from the picture of earth that you just presented to me."

"Tell us what you think it means?"

"You showed me a picture, "I said, "of an earth seething with technology and science, working with yet racing each other into ever higher levels of production. Well, I don't know whether I remembered it from something you told me in the past or from a thought you held in your mind during the presentation of the pictures you sent me earlier.

"It was the memory of a story you told me long ago. The one you mention so often about an ancient tribe of people here on earth, and their belief in something called 'The Age of Man.'"

After the long moment of silence that followed, from a feeling of spiritual love and belonging, they said, "You have come so far. At this level now, you have become one of us. Whenever you feel you are ready, you need only to take that final step. You think like we do. You are in contact with our source, the same one we use. You have earned the right, and you can make your own ascension whenever you wish."

"Does this change the rules by which we are operating?"

They said, "We will continue to operate exactly as we have in the past. You have asked if there was a limitation in the time we have to succeed in what we are doing. Bear in mind that what we are doing is the best plan. By their own negative actions, earthlings can hasten the supposedly end time many of them believe in so firmly.

"By their positive actions, they can delay any such event, and will be given more time to bring their lives into the light. There will be no change in what we are doing. It is the only method we have that can bring more of them back to the path, the path of light leading to this level of Creation.

"What we have been discussing today deals also in our

actions. Right now, your own physical body back on earth is recording everything that we say and everything we decide. What we are facing is this, unknown to you, at some time in the future we will come to the end of an epoch in the saga of man.

"Like the sinking of an ocean liner, in light with how they have lived, every person will have to sink or swim, for himself or herself. Those who have found us through this meditation, will be beginning a new age of special spirituality that will exist on a beautiful new earth for many thousand years.

"Those who are with us at that time, will cross that bridge to everlasting life and dwell in the angelic realm for eternity."

"Many believe," I said, "that earth will pass through some special cataclysmic event during this end time, Can you tell us anything about that?"

They said, "In a past paragraph, we told you that due to the irresponsible actions of man, earth was settled when it was yet immature, and needed time to mature properly. In the light of man's continued violations of the laws of nature, corrections will continue to occur on earth. in keeping with man's continued disregard for planet earth..

"What we are speaking about is the continued misuse of the planet's resources. When man learns to live in harmony with earth, it will return to its own proper balance and peace will be restored."

"Is there anything more that I can do to bring this message to the human race?"

"Just finish this book. It will help to bring our joint message to the world."

My teachers know, of course, that I am complying

with their request. through an extraordinary effort on their part to accomplish their goal.

Remember that they are working under the Divine restriction that it is the Creator's will that man be allowed to return to Creation under his own free will, and they do not view the destruction of the human body in the same tragic light as we do. Their concern is with the soul that will live again.

They tell us that if enough people will return to the path that leads to everlasting life, they will see the expanded vision that automatically follows. As they walk in the global light of God's Eternal love that guides them along the path, their own lives will return to complete harmony and perfect satisfaction.

The masters promise that if we are able to do that, with many new people being brought under the guidance of the light, their expanded influence will be felt throughout the entire world, and a natural earthly balance will be attained. Then the much feared end time catastrophe will have been avoided.

With my mind lifted into the high levels of Creation through the power of my angelic masters, I am privileged to view both sides of the problem. It is easy to see the best possible answer. That is, return to the path of light as quickly as possible.

You can then enjoy the beautiful Masters' Meditation, and allow it to take you into ever-increasing levels of spiritual consciousness. Learn the Ascension as you cross the bridge to eternity. You can then ensure your own safe passage into everlasting life

My masters have just told me, the thoughts and impressions that filled my mind during the first year of my

## Chapter XIII

study with the Tibetan Lama who called himself Tschen Li. He had begun the study of the Masters' Meditation at age 12, and used it exclusively for the remainder of his life. He had taken the vows of poverty as a child.

As he became my teacher, from the saffron color of the robe he wore, and the absence of belongings he carried, I assumed that taking those vows meant renouncing every material possession. I soon learned that although he took almost nothing with him, every physical requirement in his life mysteriously appeared when needed.

As with my spiritual teachers, they carried nothing with them, but had the entire universe of material from which to draw their needs. They lived in the angelic realm of beauty and easy access to its spirituality and Eternal Love. Once you experience it, as I and many of my advanced students already have, it's easy to remain steadfastly upon that special road back to Creation. More than that, you have the Eternal Presence to accompany you, and its love to guide you every step of the way.

While performing his many duties as a Tibetan Lama, that of physician, healer and teacher, Tschen Li used the Masters' method in all of his meditative moments. He, too, had the Eternal Presence and all of its special benefits to light his way. His vow of poverty meant only that he owned nothing, but had acquired for his use all of the materiality of the entire Cosmos.

Think of the decision I made when I allowed him to become my teacher. After years of hard work and study, I had become the master of an ocean liner, living in our own world of materiality With it I had acquired a degree of financial security. Of course, like almost everyone else,

I wished I had more.

Tschen Li traveled the sea lanes of the East with me, and often accompanied me on my visits ashore. To those who saw us ashore, we must have appeared as the Odd Couple. He walked tall and proud in his plain saffron robe. Competence and assurance surrounded him like a shield.

Suggestions of unlimited wisdom and undetectable ability completed the picture for those who dared take a second glance in his direction. Interest turned to instant respect as his powerful aura reached out and touched them. In his presence, although dressed in the uniform of a captain, no one even gave me a second glance.

This respect came to him as the result of many years of service devoted to good deeds. I learned later that he used his spare time and unusual talents in helping the less fortunate and the needy.

Others who had taken the vows of poverty, did not fare quite as well as Tschen Li. When Mataji came to him at age 12 and taught him the Masters' Meditation, he agreed to learn that meditation and, under her direction, use it instead of the Eastern method he had already learned. His long and successful life attests to its many benefits for those who use it on a regular basis.

He told me later, that his total dedication to the Masters' Meditation, carried him into benefits and abilities that no one else on earth that he knew had ever attained.

He said that after his life passed the century mark, even his closest friends seemed nervous when in his company. For he had retained his good health and had a much more youthful appearance than any of them.

At that time, this meditation had led him into unusual

high levels of spiritual contact, and to the attainment of many of the special abilities given only to the masters and the angels. He knew that he had then reached the point where he could ascend into the angelic world whenever he desired. to do so.

With these gifts came the knowledge that he could exist in comfort in any location in the universe that he cared to. Anything that he needed for his existence appeared before him with no more effort than a mere thought. The magic word here is needed, not wanted. The manifestation of his needs appeared before him in only an instant of time.

His spiritual needs were always with him through his total contact with the Eternal Presence of God. He also knew that this benefit is the birthright of every person on earth, to find this path and follow it to the position in life that he then found himself.

The advanced wisdom that came to him as the by product of this meditation, told him that as the end of the Saga of Man became increasingly evident, more and more people would cease from their earthly labors and find the path that could lead them to the same level that he had achieved.

Tschen Li had elected to remain on earth for as long as possible, and assist other ascended masters in teaching me, and helping me to bring as many others as possible onto the path before it became too late. Like Mataji and Mirva, many others among the ascended masters and angels are assisting in any way that they can.

The general opinion of many people that I meet is this: they think that there is "somebody out there," as they are prone to say, "but why don't they make a little more effort to contact me and help me to understand."

The answer to that may come as a surprise: There are many guides standing by, ready and willing to help all who ask. Surprisingly, only a few of them ever ask.

The Creator gave man, and mankind free will to live on earth as he or she desires. But with that free will comes the responsibility to ask. You have to ask first. This will explain the biblical admonition, "Ask and it will be given you. . .."

If you intentionally seek the assistance of the masters or angels, the sincerity of that request determines the degree and the extent of the assistance you will be given.

I leave it to each of you to listen to your own minds and your memories of current and past events. In the light of your understanding of what has happened in the past, make your own determination as to how well humanity is using that gift of absolute free will.

From this high level of contact, with my mind in complete contact and rapport with the Eternal Presence of the Creator, it would be easy for me to make a judgment. If I did, then my determination might very well be quite different from yours.

On tomorrow, I will again walk among you. It will be in the same physical body I have now worn for nearly eight decades. Then I will be in closer contact with the physical body, and will better understand how you, who have never known the difference, may choose to remain in the physical and continue to enjoy the only pleasures you have ever known.

It would be wise to bring to your attention, however, that when you exercise your free will, that as the result of that decision, you automatically place yourself under the

## Chapter XIII

natural law of cause and effect. Every thought and action on your part invokes a consequence that can either be positive or negative.

The Eastern world has given that consequence a name that is known and feared by them as something they know as Karma. But by whatever name you call it, the word Consequence, describes it as well as any other word you could use.

Under Universal Law, which are the perfect laws that govern the universe, it is impossible to break any of the natural laws of the universe without involving a consequence. A few examples will help you to better understand.

The law of gravity is one of those natural laws that is better understood. You could test that law by jumping from a high-flying plane without a parachute. You have come into disobedience with that law and will soon understand its natural consequence, which is almost certain death. The consequence of this law is unthinkable.

The results of other applications might be a little more subtle. If you eat more food than your body requires to sustain itself, the surplus will be stored in the fatty tissues of your body, and as a consequence you will gain weight. The consequence of eating less than your body requires will be exactly the opposite. The law of consequence is working perfectly.

King David, whom the masters tell me, was taught our meditation as a child, identified universal law in Psalm I, in his description of the Godly man ". . .whose delight was in the law of the Lord, and in that law doth he meditate both day and night." The result of David's marksmanship with a slingshot has been handed down to us through recorded history. We can conclude that he practiced for long hours in order to attain that perfection. We can also conclude from his admonition in Psalm I, that he studied this meditation with equal diligence, for he instructed everyone to meditate upon God's law both day and night.

King David spoke of God's laws with eloquence and with spiritual love. These are the unbreakable laws of the universe. The Masters' Meditation will lead you into full understanding of all of those laws.

An understanding of these laws enables you to see and understand the perfection of the universe that is all around you, and to live your life in that perfection. Thereby eliminating the awful consequences that has been so aptly described as "Hell on Earth."

Much has been written about Karma or Consequence by others who did not understand the natural laws of the universe. I find that most of what has been written flows from that misunderstanding.

An understanding of nature's laws enables you to see your place, your understanding, and every aspect of your existence in the light of the perfection of this beautiful universe of which you are a part.

The consequences of your lack of understanding may be more devastating than you could ever imagine.

When the light of the Wisdom flows to those who use the Masters' Meditation, it is easy to see examples of Karmic Consequence in the lives of almost every person that you know. Ignorance of that law is no excuse, and will not relieve you of that Consequence.

A man that I once knew well lived nearby. He had been a good man and loved his family. His wife had passed away, his grown children had gone to follow their

## Chapter XIII

own careers, and he was alone when I met him.

Retired, and with little to do, he often confessed to me that his life was aimless and unsatisfying. Yet he lived in a comfortable home, surrounded by the beauty and abundance of nature. He lived in the midst of rolling hills and tall green mountains.

A grove of stately oak trees nearby, some of them more than 200 years old, stood between him and a view of the city below him. He thoughtlessly hired a timber man to top those beautiful trees, enabling him to sit on his porch and gaze at the belching smokestacks and the consequential smog hovering over the valley below.

He often complained when his chronic gingivitis flared up with its discomfort that endured for weeks until brought under control again.

At that time, it had not been revealed to me that the inner bark from the decapitated oak trees contained an almost instant cure for his chronic pain, as well as for problems in other parts of the body.

When the Karmic Consequence of this event became clear, it might be noted that he suffered the Karmic Consequence with no knowledge that he had even broken the Law.

After he died from cancer, I remember another incident similar to the one just related. At the time the timber man cut the tops from the oak trees, he had another man cut down some beautiful mountain laurel bushes that he thought grew too close to his home. It was then that he discovered several Polk Berry bushes growing amidst the laurel. They were also cut down to wither and die.

This was a fast growing bush and came back the

following year with equal strength and size. He hired the same man to come back and dig up the bushes, root and all. I remember seeing those bushes hauled away to the incinerator in the back of the workman's pick up truck.

As my enlightenment continued, it was revealed to me that an herbal extract made from the roots of the Polk Bush, could also be used as a cure for the cancer that had brought this man's life to an early end.

The incidents that I made note of that occurred in this man's life, should not be taken as criticism. He was my friend, and I helped him in many ways. He lived his life according to his own wishes, and neither sought nor would have taken advice from me.

These incidents merely demonstrate the law of Karma and how it can occur in your life whether or not you are aware of it.

The information concerning the healing properties of herbs is not new. It was known and developed by our forefathers generations ago. It retains its full healing power today, just as it did in the past. And unlike most of today's chemical preparations, it contains little or no side effects.

All that is required is a desire to learn and know the natural laws of the universe. Wherever you look, they are there. You can find them in our libraries, gathering dust along with other tomes of almost forgotten knowledge.

With the advent of this meditation, every one of us can easily learn and use the natural laws of the universe from this perfect source, and make our lives an expression of God's will on earth. That is all you will ever need for success in this life as well as in the hereafter.

## Chapter XIV

### Students Visit Angelic Realm

Another night, another summons. As before, it came during the night. The ascension followed in the twinkling of an eye. The accelerating vibrations of light sent tingling sensations through my body as it moved into the brilliance of the angelic realm.

In but a moment of time, I found myself totally merged with the six angels, with our composite mind in total contact with the infinite mind of the Creator. The continuation of my enlightenment had already begun.

The mind of the archangel Raphael sent me a brief greeting and a welcome. Then he said, "As you are now aware, when you come with your own two teachers, I also join the group. At other times, other angels will come and work with you.

"I note that you have already brought several of your advanced students to this level. From your own point of view, tell me how you think they are progressing."

"To begin with," I said, "let us consider a scientist who has studied with me now for over three years. He comes from a group that does not consider the metaphysics worthy of their consideration. He, of course, is the exception.

"Like Einstein, his specialty involves an area of study about which very little is actually known. This special student advanced quickly through the graded series of meditation tapes and also studied personally with me occasionally.

"I made a recording of the meditation that brought him to this level. Using that tape, he comes to this level whenever he wishes. At the end of the tape, he is left in a deep silence while in total contact. While in that silence, he will ask questions related to his work and to his own private life.

"Though total dedication, he has achieved the ability at that level to receive and understand answers to those questions that come to him from the Infinite Mind. These answers contain information and suggestions that solve the problems he brought with him into these meditations."

"We know of him, and he will go far. Who else can you tell us about."

"Well", I said, "another is a business man who came to this study through my home study program. He has progressed rapidly through the graded instructions of that series. I sent him a copy of the same tape that I had made with the scientist. This student awakens an hour earlier each morning and meditates for that hour with one of our tapes.

"On the morning he used the special tape, when he went into the silence, without even asking, he was given four possible answers to a business problem that had been of concern for some time. He put those four ideas together the same day.

"Out of that, he organized a new business venture. It succeeded, and he is now president of his own company, and has become a very successful business man.

"As the result, he is prospering now, and has many employees whose salaries contribute to the wealth of that location. Not only that, but he shares his good fortune with others in his community. His life has changed for the better, and he is now a happy man.

"Not bad for a 75 year-old man, whose only salary before that was social security."

## Chapter XIV

"Thank you," Raphael said. "Remember the biblical admonition, "Thy heavenly father knoweth thy needs before thou even asketh,"

"Very well," I said. "My mother taught it to me as a child."

"We wanted to get those two unrelated incidents into the record. We know of the others also, and we are well pleased with your record."

In the moments of silence that followed, I allowed the expanded mind of the angels which I now enjoyed, to impress itself more closely into my own. They honored me with their presence and gave me the assistance I required to see the angelic realm through their eyes, just as they routinely experienced it.

After learning the lessons of the earlier meditations, the advanced students were allowed to accompany me to this level. There they began a study with the ascended masters and angels. There is only one requirement for anyone wishing to follow in their footsteps. That is to find this meditation and make it a part of their lives.

There are many so-called teachers who claim to teach you the keys to the kingdom. They have taken the position of a guru. When you follow them, you do as they say, but you never attain a level higher than their own.

The true ascension is not a group effort. True salvation is an individual effort. The Masters' Meditation is the only method that I know of where the student can transcend his own instructor and cross that bridge to eternity on his or her own with the assistance of his or her masters and guides.

Even the angels will receive you joyfully, and allow you to use their own energy and their minds, to help you view Creation as it really is. They will assist you to find your own way in the long journey to Eternity.

Earlier in this chapter, I told of the experience of two of my advanced students. On the pathway they followed in their quest for a better way of life while on earth, and the ultimate truth about eternity and everlasting life.

Only a short time has elapsed since my teachers helped me to successfully go through the near death experience. While there, they taught me how to take others by means of our Cosmic Whirlwind Meditation.

As in the near death experience, the soul has achieved a much higher level of consciousness, and become free of the physical body that is beginning to enter into a state of death. They find themselves in a tunnel through which they can ultimately ascend into eternity or return to the body if it is not yet their time.

In the Cosmic Whirlwind meditational experiences, as you learn that process as an advanced student, you master it amid all of its benefits and wonders. Your spiritual consciousness continues to advance into higher levels. At the height of these meditations, you find that since you are already in the center of that mighty whirlwind, you need only look upward to see that center, extending as a gold colored tunnel all the way to eternity.

With the aid of my masters, I have taken many others among my advanced students into the same angelic experience they gave me at that time  The results of their visits to the angelic realm would be the same or similar to the two that I explained in detail earlier.

Each of them began their journey somewhere in the past, hoping to find a meditation that would really work as I had promised them it would. Step by step, they

## Chapter XIV

moved into ever higher levels, learning the philosophy of creation and the meditation that could take them all of the way to eternity.

Ascension is not the only benefit attained from regular use of the Cosmic Whirlwind meditation. Within that special process, as if the mass of energy contained in the universe were not enough, our guides assist in a transformation of that energy into the universal life force energy. It is a force known to our masters as the Life and Love of God.

A person properly trained and attuned in the use of that energy gains access to this, the secret power of the universe. Think on that for a moment. Those who use this meditation have within their grasp the ability to alter their future existence into anything they desire

To use the description, "This is the icing on the cake of life," is but a poor and inadequate metaphor of the electrifying effect that knowledge and use of this power brings into one's existence. You are given the ability to accomplish that what you previously considered a miracle.

There are different levels of miracles. The two examples of personal success described in the beginning of this chapter, tell of people who have touched into the higher levels of access, and have momentarily paused to develop what they have already accomplished.

Once existence at that level is secure, they will go on with their advancement. The mind is part of the soul of man. Properly used, it can accomplish miracles at any stage of personal development. From the bottom to the top, which is ascension into the angelic realm, there is no limit once you enter this path back to Creation.

As with my first book, Cosmic Fire, A Guide to the

Masters' Meditation, the last chapter of this book will contain an actual meditation. It is put there to show you the actual beginning meditation. Continuing through the nine steps of the home study course in meditation will take you through increasing levels of wonder and joyful experiences. In it is the key to attaining the pleasurable wonders that await you at every level.

To sample it for yourself, have someone read it to you while you enjoy its powerful effects. Or, using your best voice, read it into a tape recorder. Relax quietly and listen to your recorded voice. Form a picture in your mind of each scene that voice describes. You can then experience for yourself, the joy and the beauty of the meditation.

It is all there, waiting for you to begin the most important step you will ever take to change your life for the better.

## Chapter XV

### The Masters' Meditation and Reiki

When I began studying the Masters' Meditation, I entered into a powerful inner experience through that process which the masters and the angels claimed for their own. It welcomed me with the gentle embrace of the Creator's presence and love, then lifted me into a soul-satisfying interlude I wanted to continue forever.

In addition to its special contents, such as philosophy and wisdom, it carried me into instant spiritual contact with ever higher levels of consciousness and awareness.

Personal contact with the inner world came during the first lesson. The intensity of the experience deepened with each succeeding meditation. New plateaus that I reached during each meditation were lasting intervals of joy, as the soul prepared for the next step upward and into ever higher dimensions.

Among its many special benefits, and nestling close to the meditation, lay a powerful additional benefit my teachers called the Masters' Healing. The combined benefit of these two forces produced dynamic results.

The sincere meditator found life becoming more balanced, enjoyable, and filled with healing energies at the same time. Overall improvement of general health continued in pace with increasing spiritual vibrations. The path back to Creation became a delightful intervening period of delight that expanded beyond the meditative process. It continued into daily activities that followed, making them less fatiguing and more productive.

Extracted from the Masters' Healing process of this meditation, a new method of healing migrated from Japan to our Western world during the seventies. It went by the name of Reiki, which means universal energy. It should not have been called "new," since its parent, The Masters' Meditation, came into being with the creation of the angels, back in the very beginning of time.

To make Reiki more easily taught in our world, it used only a small part of the healing process of the meditation. Even the meditative process, which is the power source of the process, somehow remained behind.

Without the meditation, it came to us as only a bare boned process, lacking even the disciplined mind of the Oriental, and the intense concentration required to master any subject that came before them.

With the meditation, and the disciplined mind and the spiritual or universal energy that it produces, Reiki could become a powerful force for good. As it is today, without the meditation and discipline, it has become weakened and almost ineffectual, except for an occasional teacher who possesses natural spiritual abilities and combines them with the Reiki he or she teaches.

To give you a quick background of the subject as it came to me from the Oriental World, Mataji and Mirva, my two beloved teachers, have been spiritual custodians and teachers of the meditation for untold centuries. Mataji taught it to Tschen Li when he was 12 years old, and a chela or student in a monastery of Tibet.

Tschen Li taught it to me for 32 years, beginning at the end of World War II. Much earlier he had taught it to a Japanese Monk named Mikao Usui in Tibet, who took it back with him to Japan.

Tschen Li, sadly informed me that Usui died in Japan in 1915. From that incident, Tschen Li knew that Usui had not embraced the Masters' Meditation completely. If

## Chapter XV

he had, he could have lived a much longer and useful life.

From Tschen Li's total dedication to the Masters' Meditation, he liked it so well he used it instead of the Eastern method. He lived among dedicated users of the Eastern Meditation. They lived only the normal span of life for the area. His lifetime far exceeded theirs. Tschen Li lived on earth well into the latter part of his second century.

He then made his ascension and, from that level, now assists those in the angelic realm in their efforts to bring this meditation to others. He still contacts and works with me, helping in my own teachings.

Reiki was brought to our world in the 1970's by Hawaii Takata, a Hawaiian born American citizen of Japanese lineage. She learned it from a Japanese doctor who had learned it from Dr. Usui much earlier. While she used Reiki's healing energy in Hawaii during World War II and for a period thereafter, because of that war, she did not feel free to begin teaching it until much later.

Meanwhile, I had finished my long period of study and internship with the meditation, and began teaching it at about the same time.

Then one of my students took a Reiki class with Mrs. Takata. She became attracted to his energy while he sat quietly in his chair during lunch-break, in a deep state of meditation. She later asked him where he had learned such a powerful meditation. She knew nothing about me, but when he told her I had studied under a Tibetan Lama named Tschen Li, she apparently knew of his fame, and immediately contacted me.

Our beginning contacts were mainly by long distance telephone. She had many teaching engagements. So did

I. That method had to suffice for over a year before we could meet.

Everything in our activities bordered on the unusual, even the first time we met. I had just finished a week end seminar in South Florida, and returned home to relax and meditate. She unexpectedly called me from the Miami airport, and arrived at my place an hour later.

During our earlier conversations, we had covered much of the preliminary information. Now it was down to the business of teaching her the meditation and exchanging what we each knew about the attunement process of Reiki and about the vital life force that went under the common name of universal energy.

Much too early, her limousine returned, signaling the time had come to return to the airport. We had only covered part of what she wanted to know, and agreed to meet again as soon as we could. The next meeting never came to pass. I finally learned she had passed through transition a few months later.

From what information we had exchanged, and the exchange of energy between us as we shared attunements with each other, I knew the level to which her Japanese teacher had taken her as he taught her Reiki. She showed me the level of the attunement she had given other teachers she had made, that gave them authority to teach the First and Second levels or degrees of Reiki to others.

In the early eighties, in an effort to determine the extent of their Reiki knowledge, I took classes under some of those teachers, and found they were already changing the process to suite their own interpretation and understanding. While I feel sure that some may have adhered to the strict guidelines they had learned, I had to bite my tongue and say nothing in some of the classes.

As with the meditation, you cannot alter the purity of the masters' teaching without losing some of its effect. If you continue the masters will withdraw their support.

We have now reached the third and fourth generation among those who became teachers under some of the original teachers who studied under Mrs. Takata. From what I see now, the purity of the process has suffered. What some are teaching now bears little resemblance to the original. Yet some of them paid a handsome price for that privilege.

For a three-year period during those early years, I did not allow myself to be associated with what Reiki had become. Teaching the Masters' Meditation required my full-time dedication. Then I received a letter from one of those Reiki teachers. Under our home study program, she had studied the meditation for over three years. An excellent student, she progressed rapidly through the entire course.

As she moved into the higher levels of the meditation, which is the source of power under which Reiki exists, it had restored part of the original energy to the Reiki she used. As the result of the meditation, her Reiki had come alive. With that missing ingredient to draw from, her work became a pleasure. She began to share her new-found energy with the less fortunate.

With her permission, I quote the following excerpts from her letter:

"My Reiki work has expanded and has so enriched my life by use of these tapes. It is truly a miracle. When I even touch now, I am sensing the pain felt by the other person.

"As I do the initiations, the love of God for them is so overwhelming for them and myself also, I can hardly describe it in human terms. The love is also present as I do Reiki healings. I touch and that electricity runs through my body, one knows they are connected.

"The tapes have meant so much to me. My Reiki practice has expanded to treatment of persons who are much more ill than those I treated before. Is it because of this unconditional love of God? There is so much that I don't understand, but I don't question because God is truly such a part of my life.

"Anyhow, my eternal thanks for your precious tapes."

What a beautiful letter! It makes me give thanks to the masters for their efforts in teaching me the entire process, and thankful they selected me to become their message bearer.

Other Reiki teachers, who work with me in our meditation classes, have had similar results. They ask me to teach them the part of the program they feel is missing. I have begun to teach them the missing parts of the process, exactly as the masters taught me. This gives them the assurance that they have found the original teaching. Their attitude and teaching ability has improved.

Those who study the Masters' Meditation with me soon learn that it and the Master's Healing process are the same process that was taught to Dr. Usui by Tschen Li back around the turn of the last century. In some of my letters I only state that the Masters' Meditation will enhance Reiki and other healing methods.

Universal Life Force Energy, a more complete name for Universal Energy, was infused in all living things early

## Chapter XV

in the beginning of creation. Its force is the essence of all living matter. It enables humanity to grow, to move around in the sense of changing location, and to enjoy all other gifts the Creator made available to us.

Unfortunately for us, the gift of free choice stands between us and the full utilization and enjoyment of this, the greatest of all gifts we received. For within that life force that is showered down upon us in great abundance, comes the Life and the Love of God.

It is like a child in rebellion against the wisdom of a well-meaning parent. With no thought of consequence, it seeks only to satisfy present desires. My teachers show me the same attitude prevailing in almost all of humanity today. In satisfying only their physical appetites, they eat the wrong food, create destructive personal habits, and submerge the vital life force within themselves with a harmful debris that all but suffocates the gift of life

Reiki can help bring the life force energy into its proper balance. The full force of the Masters' Meditation, with its ability to produce an unlimited supply of that vital life force energy, can restore perfect balance with an abundant of energy to spare. When you realize that this seemingly simple meditation can produce such dramatic results, and put it to work in your life, you are well on the path back to Creation. Would you want to settle for anything less?

To understand Universal Energy, you have to begin with the results obtained in the first meditation we teach. In it you soon see that there is no vacant space anywhere in Creation. Every bit of that space is filled with a golden mist. The angels call it Cosmic Fire, and tell us that it is God's presence everywhere in Creation. So it is no coincidence the name of my first book is *Cosmic Fire*.

Out of that Cosmic Fire God created the vital life force and imbued every living thing with that force in a great abundance. It is the essence of that precious force that enables us to come alive physically, mentally and spiritually, and live amid the splendor of all there is.

There is a perfection in living in the full glory of Creation, and in the manner intended by the perfect mind that made it all possible. We were also intended to one day find these angelic masters, and use their teachings to lead us back to full contact of the Creation from which we all came.

This meditation is the masters' road back. The first part of the meditation puts us in contact with that special energy. It makes us feel good. We use it with pleasure, not knowing it is only a beginning.

Half way along this path, we have advanced to a higher level where we are introduced to a meditation that enables us to use our minds and our bodies to co-create that energy in any amount we choose, and to share it with every living thing on earth

No longer do we have to spend an entire lifetime in silent contemplation, waiting for inner contact to begin. In our special process, we sit quietly in a blissful meditation, while we surround and fill ourselves with unlimited quantities of the healing energies of that precious life force. There is no limit. We have sufficient energy to fill our every need, and enough left over to fill the needs of every other living thing on planet earth.

This is not something reserved for only a few of the lucky ones. It is available to every soul on earth who feels inclined to ask.

## Chapter XVI

### Mother Mary Appears

Each meditation contains one or more unexpected incidents. Our masters use this to continue teaching us the unlimited avenues of learning available. There is no limit. As a reward for having attained this level, they have given us free access to the almost unattainable repository containing all of the knowledge of the universe.

The following incident is explained in detail, under the direction and at the insistence of the masters and angels. It involves personal spiritual contact with a very high level angelic person who came to earth years ago for a special purpose. I deeply love and honor this person, and present the account with her approval, only to advise the world of the precarious conditions threatening planet earth at this time. Also to let those who use our meditation know the infinite possibilities and benefits it gives to those who use it. This chapter would not have been written otherwise. . .

After my advanced extension students learn of these possibilities, they may want to try to do the same thing. It can put them in touch with that unlimited source of information.

In my last book, I wrote about a gifted student we referred to as Magnolia. She had learned to speak while in an intense state of meditation. It has happened so often in our past meditations, we now accept it as normal. After learning this meditation, many others have achieved the same ability, but seldom even think to try.

In my own near death experience, my teachers showed me their way to cross the bridge separating us from the angelic realm. The powerful Masters' Meditation can spiritually take us across that bridge with the aid of our masters. While there, with expanded mind and consciousness, the wonders of that promised land are ours to explore

Every spare moment of my time finds me with one or more of my teachers, studying the wonders of Creation. They tell me I have my own place in the continuing saga of ever-expanding universes within the cosmos. Once you find this level, none of earth's pleasures could ever suffice. They pass away too soon and are forgotten. The joy, ecstasy and rapture we experience at this level never ends. We know they will be ours to enjoy throughout eternity.

Time and space have no limitations for the mind and soul attuned to the angelic world. The ascended masters attained that level as the natural result of past lifetimes on earth. In their concern for humanity, they work with the angels to lead us back to the path of light. When the full light of the Eternal Presence fills us with its love, nothing earth has to offer could ever satisfy us again. When you have it all, there is no need for more..

This meditation began in the usual manner. Under the guidance of our teachers, Magnolia and I quickly made our spiritual ascension. Our teachers greeted us and led us to our seats in my private box in what passes for the opera house on the planet New Home. They placed me in my usual seat. Magnolia sat on my right. Mataji sat in front, facing me, and Mirva beside me on my left. Magnolia's two teachers took similar positions, one in front and one on her right.

The vacant chair between the two teachers in front of us told me a special visitor would come during this session. On the previous night, visions of a heavenly face and glistening white robe heralded the presence of Mother

## Chapter XVI

Mary again in our midst. Memories of her past visits reminded me of the heavenly moments those meetings brought to us. Her prophetic revelations were powerful and always important to the needs of the present.

Magnolia sat quietly beside me. The stillness of her posture betrayed an attentive readiness. The many times we had been here in the past had alerted her to expect information and guidance that would be of powerful importance to us and to all of humanity in general.

Heightening vibrations filled the room around us, signaling the arrival of another holy presence in our midst. The radiant figure of Mother Mary materialized slowly in the chair facing us. Her beautiful face shone brightly in the reflection of her golden aura that glistened brightly about her, tingeing her immaculate white robe with a gilded hue.

She was at home and at peace in the midst of the angels and masters. I sensed the swift mental exchange of greetings between them. She looked at me and smiled in recognition, then sent a beam of golden light to reflect upon Magnolia, who still sat quietly, waiting for what was to come or for permission to speak.

Since my voice had led Magnolia to this level, I said quietly: "And now, the beautiful Mother Mary has graced us with Her presence. I want you to open your mind to embrace the mind of Mother Mary. Feel the blessings flowing from the mind of the Mother of the Universe. The love that you feel embraces and is in tune with all of the knowledge of the universe.

"Ask Mother Mary how we can best help earth, based on her concept of earth at this time. I ask that you begin telling us any special messages are receiving.

MAGNOLIA: "I feel such a depth. It is difficult to

describe. It as if I am experiencing being within the womb. I feel such a loving presence. I feel myself being drawn toward her. almost as if I am experiencing motherhood and infancy simultaneously.

"I feel myself being lifted even above the spiritual guidance to join them and look at something. She is reminding me of a past meditation where we saw Creation. She is reminding me that we need to keep that creative force, and the awareness of that creative force at all times. And that each human that has experienced earth is capable of understanding creation and the creative forces in the universe. And the terminology that is bantered in our society as being born again, the purification process is in fact a very spiritual process. And it can be painful because it indicates change.

"She says that the earth itself is going through a birth, if you will, but one of our tasks at this time is to assist in the birth, or rebirth, if you will. All of these things that are happening on the earth plane is an indication of a difficult birth, and that we can assist through our meditations, and in a sense be midwives for the earth.

"But love, and working with the creative forces is critical right now. A sense of urgency without danger. The earth will be reborn. How smoothly the transition takes place depends on all of us. There are forces at work to make it easier, and forces that are making it harder. It is not something that they put a time line on in the spiritual sense, but the process has begun.

"Mother Mary is with us, and will be with us throughout the whole process. She is, in a sense, the spiritual midwife, and she needs our help, needs it in the sense to ease the birth or the rebirth of this planet.

## Chapter XVI

Working with the energies, and allowing it to happen, with our efforts surrounding the earth constantly with light and love, keeping the connection strong between love and the creative forces.

"She mentions quarantine earlier. The earth is very vulnerable right now. The transformation is, and as it is happening, it's being recreated almost every day. It is a sense of waiting. But each time there is, shall we say, a convulsion in the birth process, and it's hard to visualize the earth as both a mother and a child. The transformation is more like a, shedding a skin, yet it's also superimposed with the mother and the child being born from the mother. And yet they are one and the same.

"But this new life form, this new entity, Gaia, Earth, will have a higher vibrational energy, will be different from the old earth. It's a very interesting sensation. It's going through the process all within itself.

"All of these changes climatically, all of these alterations with the physiology, the earthquakes. They are negative energies being relieved, that are being picked up by different cultures. The wars are all a part of that. The cleansing is happening. And the earth is vulnerable.

"Mother Mary is there to help guide, in a loving way, all of the spiritual energies that encompass the earth. She is in constant vigilance, radiating her love. This is her purpose When she manifested and became the mother of Jesus, in a sense she was preparing herself for this role.

"The main focus of this now is, she is reaching out to us to be aware of the process, and to assist in it as much as possible. Tapping into the creative force of the universe, the cosmic whirlwind, Surrounding the earth, the planet with our energies in the physical realm. We need to continue, and have others continue, to keep this transformation in our hearts and minds, to give it energy, to give it love, to give it light, to contribute to the ease of the passage. In the sense that there is nothing set in stone, there is no predestined goal, because this is a process that can be changed by our energies, can be altered by the energies that exist on this earth plane.

She is saddened by the difficult birth that she sees, and she can only assist from the spiritual plane. And it is up to us, here on this earth plane, to work with her and with the energies, to assist it to be an easier birth. Our societies, our cultures have brought a lot of negative energies into the earth, in a physical sense. All of the changes that we have made physically have contributed to the difficult birthing process, or the hindrance or the negative aspects of the birthing.

"She is conveying an image to me of what it could have been, just so I would know how easy it could have been. A very easy birth if spiritually we had been more advanced as a race of humanity. But, because we do have, shall we say, illnesses in a spiritual sense within our race, it is causing some difficulties with the rebirth of the planet. And she is telling me the finality because she thinks it will connect with a lot of people, that it will help them to see that it is something that is happening both within us, and without simultaneously.

"As we evolve, so does the earth evolve. And it's this evolution that is causing the rebirth of the planet. In time, both in a physical sense and a spiritual sense. The vibrations have all converged to add to this process. It didn't start the process, but it's just the right time within the Cosmic Consciousness that this planet evolves.

## Chapter XVI

"And that is why she's here. And that is why she feels the urgency to reach out to us. To work with us. Raphael is very much involved because birthing and healing are very strongly interwoven. Particularly in this case it's being a rebirth of this planet, it's also a healing.

"I am seeing two images simultaneously of two different earths that we could see in the future. And I am not frightened by the difference. It's intriguing. On one side I see an earth that's very dark. It's one, I guess, that you would see in a science fiction narrative that would be the more negative, the more fearful, the more cloud-covered . It doesn't seem to radiate light from the inside. It looks ill. There's not a lot of colors, and the colors there are dull. It's a sad and wistful earth.

"But on the other side I am seeing this orb of light where the colors are brilliant. Everything seems clear. The clouds are even clear  It's a classic of illness and health. And what we are doing is trying to find the balance. We are trying to find the point that is the best possible transition for the earth that we live on.

"It could go in either direction. If we would only start meditating, and you know that's hardly possible for everyone, but if people did nothing and just gave up, it would become darkness. But we must continue to struggle toward the light so that the transition will result in a planet that's been reborn, that radiates light as well as receives light.

"And now I am seeing that the apex of these two images are almost like an arrow going out to a balanced earth that's in between. And that on that earth there's still going to be strife. I don't know that it's going to be possible at this point for us to achieve that radiant light.

It's almost as if I'm perceiving that this is not the last transition earth will go through. But it's a movement in the direction toward light. That we have been in spiritual darkness. And that as we draw light unto ourselves, we will be radiating it to the earth. And alternately all beings on the earth will radiate a light that will contribute to peace.

RALPH: "Ask Mother Mary what would happen if more and more people would begin to practice this meditation and come to the same higher levels themselves. Would that help?"

MAGNOLIA; "Almost assuredly. The guides and the masters are working fervently for that purpose.

"She again gives the analogy of a mother giving birth. If the mother that is giving birth is stress free, and will act in tune with her body, in tune with the world around her in an environment where she feels comfortable, loved, nurtured. Then even if the birth is a difficult one. all is well. If, on the other hand, she isn't comfortable, she feels tension around her, it becomes more difficult. The birthing process takes longer, and could have the same result, a positive result. But it makes the birth process take longer and be more difficult.

"What she is saying to me is that the more people that participate and embrace this concept, and meditate and work with their guides and masters to provide more light and love on this earth plane, it will most definitely help. There's no doubt there."

RALPH: "This has been a very beautiful conversation and contact with Mother Mary. And I can sense the masters that surround us now, and I can sense the radiance that moves out and surrounds us all, and the

## Chapter XVI

Eternal Presence of God just extended and infusing our beings with its love. And we're in contact. We are beginning to spread this throughout the entire earth, this Love and the Eternal Presence of God. And perhaps we can make a breakthrough. And I thank you for your contact today. And I thank Mother Mary who came to me and told me to arrange it. And she has imparted a tremendous amount of information. Is there anything further she would like to say?"

MAGNOLIA: "She is asking that we do this on a regular basis. That the contact has been made, and she is asking that we continue this contact. She is also saying that she will be with us at all times. And because this is such an important thing, that the meditations that we enter into, each time we enter, to visualize what you have directed. That as we feel the Golden Mist and the Golden Light around us, to continue to have that to encompass the earth itself. The earth needs protection. The earth is vulnerable. All of the negative thought forms are within it are like cancerous growths that need to be healed and soothed. That the more of us that can incorporate this in our daily meditations, the greater help it will be.

"Because we are part of the earth. The earth is a part of us. We tend to think of us as being other than ourselves but in fact it is within us. And by healing ourselves. healing in our daily meditations, healing the earth along with ourselves, we are accelerating the birth process in a very positive way.

"And now she is bowing to us, and thanking us."

RALPH: "She is beautiful. Well are you ready to start coming back now."

MAGNOLIA: "Oh-h-h-h-h-h yes-s-s-s-s-s!"

On that note, I brought the meditation to an end. She and I sat in silence for a long time. The Eternal Presence surrounded and covered us with Its love. Our bodies remained relaxed, tingling with excitement. Our minds filled with love and memories of the intense pleasure of our spiritual contact with the holy Presence.

We both slowly returned to an almost awakened awareness, My mind centered on the vivid description of planet earth and its inhabitants we had just shared. No words broke the meditative silence around us. None was needed. Her concern for our planet fully matched that of mine. The thoughts conveyed to us from the mind of Mother Mary weighed heavily upon me.

Magnolia sat quietly at my right side. Our minds were in complete harmony. Although we had not as yet developed telepathy, I knew that the message she had just received raced throughout her mind, giving her many things to reflect upon while in this deep altered state of awareness.

Memory of the vision of Mother Mary's presence had left us in the deep state ecstasy. Past experience taught us that it would remain for a prolonged period of time.

The masters had taught me to conduct an entire meditative session, and speak the words that carried others into meditation while deep in the same intense state of meditation as those around me.

The minds of Mataji and Mirva joined mine. They said, "She needs to rest. You also can relax a little, but hold your mind open. We still have other things to discuss.

This session will be continued in the next chapter.

## Chapter XVII

### Mother Mary Continues

In the meditative silence that continued, my thoughts shifted rapidly between the startling events of the past hour. In reality as in the area of meditative contact, the quiet form of Magnolia remained in a deep state of meditation while seated beside me. As my mind reached out to determine the depth of her inner contact, the combined mind of my two teachers sent me a message. "She's still in a deep sleep," they said. "Give her a little more time to adjust to her recent contact with the mind and presence of Mother Mary."

Their thoughts had intensified the warm glow of the Eternal Presence surrounding us. Other masters and the angels remained with us, adding their energy to that of our group.

I had taped Magnolia's actual words as she described her contact with Mother Mary, and the messages she spoke as they were given to her during the meeting. They have now been reproduced verbatim in the account of this session to allow the reader to share the actual scene with us, and to draw his or her own conclusions as to the meaning of this angel's words.

"What more can I do?" I heard my mind say. The question directed to no one in particular.

I should have remembered that mental contact with my angelic teachers remained open. Mataji said, "We feel your sadness over what Mother Mary's said. Her assessment of the condition of earth at this time is shared by many at this level of awareness."

"Thank you," I said. "I desperately need advice. You know this meditation can make a difference. Mother Mary agreed with you. Can you tell me what I can do to bring this message to the attention of more people, before it's too late?"

"You have the answer in your hands right now," she said. "Finish your book and publish it."

"They tell me that getting a book published is like having a baby. It takes at least nine months from the time it's accepted. Do we have that much time?"

"You have grown accustomed to being in our presence." she said. "You accept it and take it for granted. Perhaps you haven't detected the powerful energy that has just come to help us."

"If you mean Mother Mary, I am aware of the energy she can bring with her help?"

"More than that," she said. "The powerful archangel Raphael has added his help to our group. His assigned area of activity has been with the healing energy from this level that he sends to earth as a gift to humanity. There is another large group of angels working with him. Mother Mary has worked with him in this endeavor for a long time. Remember that she also came into our group with him on a full time basis this morning."

"The Masters' Healing," I found myself saying, as I almost jumped out of my chair, "and it's an integral part of the Masters' Meditation. What an unbeatable combination! With the two of them working together, we could change the world."

"Have you noticed the increase in requests for information and instructions in the healing part of the meditation?"

"Yes," I said, "there has been an increase."

"When they read our book," she said, "it will become

## Chapter XVII

an avalanche. Will you be ready?"

"Several advanced students have offered to help," I said. "We can increase our staff as it becomes necessary. I'm glad to have both of your groups at my side to help."

"Don't forget Raphael and Mary," she said. "We are now working together as one group, but much larger. If we are to succeed it will take a mutual effort among all of us, and your full cooperation from the earth plane."

"You already have that," I said, "As earth's condition worsens, many of our people are growing concerned. They are looking for something that will be of help, but they can't find anything they feel confident to accept. Can you think of anything else we can do that can help us in that direction?"

She said, "Many programs are now offered by others to the people of your world. In turn, they become disappointed when they feel no different and there is no noticeable benefit as has been promised.

"You should consider reminding everyone that the benefits from our meditation are felt immediately. They really work every time, and will produce the results we promise. The biblical expression, 'By their deeds ye shall know them,' explains it perfectly.

"Apart from Mother Mary appearing before a large crowd and speaking to them directly, and we would never do that, the powerful results of our program are the best evidence of their value.

"You should also speak about the special contacts with important people that are made possible at the highest level of the meditation. We know that Mother Mary recently came to you personally, while you were in your own meditation. She had to come to you and offer her services before you acted. Tell us about that.?"

"You are correct, of course," I said. "You should know the answer better than I. You have been in contact with me for most of my life. It made my life easier and more pleasant. People who come to me by referral from one of my students are already aware of the nature of my teaching. When I tell a new group the nature and details, I sense their amazement and evidence of some disbelief.

"Our process is far reaching and powerful. As words of description and explanation fall from my lips, it even amazes me to hear what I am saying. At those times, you know that I have to call upon you for extra energy to help me through a difficult lecture.

"You are with me during my contacts with important people from earth's past. You taught me that the history of the universe is available to those who have reached the higher levels of our meditation. Speaking with those powerful individuals is part of my ever-expanding learning process. I have conversed with so many of them I have lost count. Any advanced student can be taught to do the same thing. Let me tell you now how simple it is.

"As in the case of Mother Mary coming to me, my wife and I were returning home from an event. She drove the car. I sat on the front seat beside her. As my eyes closed for a moment's rest, a sudden surge of energy enveloped me. I sensed your presence when the face of Mother Mary appeared in my mind. I went with her, and we sat together on a sofa in a place I took to be her home.

"She greeted me warmly, then told me her concern for our planet if humanity continued to live in disobedience of the laws of God. She knew of my student Magnolia, and asked that I bring her to one of our meditative sessions as

## Chapter XVII

soon as possible. Magnolia agreed, and we told of the first session in the last chapter. They agreed upon having several future sessions, and the results of those sessions being put into a book to be written as soon as possible. I agreed to conduct the sessions that would make those meetings possible.

"I asked about her son, Jesus, for he had not visited us in some time. She replied that He was having a period of contemplation in his concern over so many people on earth misusing his name for monetary purposes. She did not elaborate, but for the information of anyone who finds it of interest, I present this in our book in the same words She gave them to me.

"I have had your instructions on how to write about my meeting with you and other masters and angels. Writing about the others is a new experience for me and you will have to tell me whether or not, as well as how to do that."

They had listened intently, Mataji said. "We will know when you write it. Mother Mary has already told you to write of this meeting, and asked Magnolia to put the messages contained in the remaining sessions into a book. She wants the world to know her conception of the conditions troubling earth at this time, and her predictions of what will occur if they are not changed.

"Tell us in a few words what we have to do?" I asked. "I have just switched on my recorder, and will print your actual words."

She said, "We have thoroughly covered that problem in previous chapters. If enough people learn this meditation, and practice it regularly, it will be the best way we know to correct the imbalance that may some day destroy the world."

"Tell me again how this meditation can help."

"You have stated the benefits of our meditation earlier in this book. Briefly, with regular practice it will bring one's life into perfect balance. Healing energy begins to flow within with the first session. The added energy improves the quality of life.

"Contact with higher levels of spiritual consciousness eliminates the negative effect of disbelief. It replaces that with positive beliefs flowing out of the glorious spiritual love of Creation that abounds in those higher levels of consciousness.

"Continued contact with those delightful levels of consciousness opens one's awareness to the natural laws of the universe. Intimate contact with that love makes the laws of Creation easily understood. Among them the law of consequence becomes clear. For every action there is a consequential reaction.

"Awareness of the unavoidable negative reaction to negative actions within one's life, stimulates the desire to avoid any negative reaction that would "mess up my life," as one of your students so aptly told you.

"The natural results of cleaning up one's thinking works in two ways: it first manifests in an attitudinal change in behavior and life style to one of thoughtful consideration of one's own life and the natural consequence of how it is lived. Secondly, the same responsible attitude reflects outward to one's understanding of the world in which they must exist. And the world will take notice of one more individual that cares.

"Others will notice when a friend or acquaintance makes such a noteworthy change in attitude. Some of

## Chapter XVII

those of importance around them will follow the lead. One by one, each new meditator adds his or her energy to the love of self and the love of nature.

"If you can get enough people to read our book, we can change some of the destructive attitudes to the point that we can save our world from chaos and destruction."

And it is to this end that I have resolved to dedicate the remainder of my life here on planet earth.

Through this meditation, the masters and angels have clearly shown me the next and final step. It will begin for me when I follow the example of my former teacher, Tschen Li, as well as the many other ascended masters who preceded him.

At the proper time for them, they crossed the bridge to eternity. In one final step, they began the blissful journey that led them, and will lead others, into everlasting life.

In the simple meditative journey through the Masters' Meditation, you can do the same.

This can be likened to opening the door to knowledge. The meditative contact with Mother Mary continues on a regular basis. In addition, in our regular meditations she adds her voice and manifests her concern for our planet and its people. She merges her energy with that of my masters, and some students report they are aware of her presence and of her concern.

In our special meditations with her, she asks us to emphasize her concern for earth and its inhabitants to everyone that is mutually interested in the problem. We should ask them to pass the word on to others, and ask them to do the same.

We have many meditators working with us at this

time.  Not all of them have reached the higher levels. Each level gives the student intense satisfaction. We find that the normal attitude of this group is to enjoy its bliss and thoroughly master that level before proceeding on to the next,

While each level is filled with magical experiences that fill the soul with the joy of ascension, each one increases the flow of energy within that enables them to excel in any level of achievement they desire.  The great breakthrough comes with the attainment of the sixth level, the cosmic whirlwind.

It is at that level that they are introduced to the secret power of the universe, and achieve the ability to co-create the life force energy that is the gift of God.  This is the energy that Jesus referred to when he said, "One person standing forth for God could change the whole world."

Mother Mary has said that as few as 10 of the most advanced at that level, meditating in concert and jointly spreading that energy over the face of the earth, could override the negativity the billions thoughtlessly and unknowingly create.  Even fewer that 10 can stop the downward slide and give us another chance to reverse the trend.  Of course, we need all of the help we can get.

My teachers tell me that this is our last and best chance.  Join with us today.  Add your energy to that of our own.  Is this not a worthy goal for every thinking person on earth?

## Chapter XVIII

### Mona

From out of a deep sleep, the delightful energies of ascension came and surrounded my body, then lifted me swiftly into the familiar sensations of space travel. When the outline of the planet New Home loomed into view, I looked beyond to my customary meeting place with my spiritual teachers. They had summoned me again for consultation and teaching.

Mataji and Mirva greeted me from their usual lounge chairs as I settled into my own, nestling comfortably in between them, feeling their loving presence embrace me. Special energies of harmonium welcomed my arrival, adjusting my own with sensations of belonging.

As usual, their inner thoughts had intensified the warm glow of the Eternal Presence that welcomed me into their midst. Other masters and the angels had come to add their thoughts and energy to that of our group.

I had already sensed an element of finality in the group mind that occasionally touched my own, and wondered if this was only a final wrap-up to the message they wanted the world to hear through their book, or if it foreshadowed something worse.

I often wished I had attained the total telepathy the masters and angels enjoyed. But until some future day I took that final step into their world, happiness meant accepting the limited mental contact they gave me. The surprised look on the faces of my two teachers, told me they had received the previous thought.

Mataji said, "From all we have shared together, why should there be doubt?"

"The something worse in the previous thought was

incomplete," I said. "To have completed it, would be an indication of doubt in my mind suggesting that we would not succeed in our mission. For that reason I stopped it before it became complete. Look ahead to the next thought, where I wished for total telepathy between us, and found total happiness in what you have already given me."

"You dreamed of our villa just before we called you this morning," came the combined thought. "We know you picket it up from the others."

"Thanks for including my wife," I thought, "and also for helping her grow and learn so quickly. Her assistance helps me meet my teaching schedule. It gives me time to write and teach more efficiently.

"The others you mentioned took us to New Home yesterday, thinking you had already told us of the new village you prepared for us. We almost never mention the others in our book, but they work with us always."

"So does your wife," they said. "With Mona, Scarlet and Flika, the angels refer to us as the quintet. They will be with us in what we plan for you today."

Scarlet and Flika are the affectionate names Erna and I gave two angelic guides that work with us closely and are always available when we call. Appearing in the full dress of angels, in my recent near death experience, they guided me through the tunnel of light leading to the angelic realm.

They are the angels that almost always appear, standing on either side of Mataji as she leads me and our students through the meditations. At other times, Mirva and Mona perform that duty.

In all meditations, Rupon and the Master Healer come

## Chapter XVIII

from the Temple of Lights and assist with the meditations. From the angelic realm, my old friend Tschen Li stands ready to help in any way he can.

And all of them are ready to help the students of the angelic home study course they allow me to present to the world. In this case, please remember that one has to plan his or her time, and really work with their guides, and call for their assistance. In other words, they really have to ask for help, even though they may not have yet learned to see or hear them.

The chairs in front of us gave way to an open, stage like floor. My two masters and I sat front and center, in the first row. Many angels filled the rows of seats behind. The lights dimmed. A spotlight from above formed a small circle in center stage before us.

Spiritual vibrations hummed softly, filled the room with sensations and promises of things yet to come, and sent tingling vibrations up and down my entire being.

The Eternal Presence of Creation descended upon us with magnificent splendor, fortifying me for an ancient ritual of purification perhaps, known only to the few who have reached this level.

The last thought brought an instant response. They said, "It's a new meditation for you now. One you can teach your most advanced students later. It's one we most often use to welcome new ascended masters as they come to us from earth. You will find it intensely powerful and useful.

"Watch the stage in front of you. It is beginning."

A beautiful angel floated downward, in the center of the beam of light entering the room from above. A robe of glistening white adorned her slender body, reflecting the golden aura that surrounded her. The angelic face of our beloved guide, Mona, shone through the golden halo that encircled her head, setting my own body aglow with anticipation.

A consummate actress, her highly regarded reputation extended out through the major population centers of the angelic universe. She had been with me for many years. We felt fortunate she preferred to remain with our group.

Moving to front center stage, her lustrous blue eyes fixed steadfastly upon mine. Her body, arms and hands began a slow rhythmic movement that resembled the early morning Tai Chi rituals Tschen Li had shown me so often in China.

Only those familiar with the power symbols of the universe could have recognized the pattern. Every stroke of those powerful symbols executed by those dazzling hands, sent corresponding surges of energy from each special move into every part of my body.

I sat there in a daze. Each movement brought me into a deepening state of rapture, with the accompanying desire to float blissfully away into some fanciful episode of everlasting life. Her eyes held mine. I could not close them, no matter how hard I tried.

The hand and arm movement continued as step by step, she moved backward to center stage. With Mataji and Mirva holding my arms, I found my feet moving across the stage, following Mona to the center, almost without being aware of it.

Her hand movements stopped as I moved close in front of her, almost touching. She reached out and held my hands. Mataji stood in front of me, close to my right shoulder, Mirva on my left. Their hands rested lightly on my shoulders. Scarlet and Flika joined the other angels that came to fill the remaining space around me. Standing close, their auras played delightful tunes on the tensing nerves and muscles within me.

They had said this was the usual method of welcome for newly arrived ascended masters from earth. I felt honored to receive the same treatment. Since we had only begun, I knew the best was yet to come.

As before, the light bodies of the angels merged into mine, The energy of eight powerful angels joined mine in forming a composite body that my consciousness accepted as my own. Their minds joined mine in the same manner, forming a composite mind, with my mind the main focus of the others.

Infinite understanding of the universe flowed into my mind as the infinite mind of the universe embraced me. At this level, with a mind that embraced the cosmos enjoying sensations of omniscience and the other senses expanded in proportion, I felt a quick word of caution from Mataji's mind. "Just look," she warned. "Don't even think. You are only here to see and learn."

"Then take me back," I said.

"No," she said. "Just remember everything you have experienced. The final part is beginning now. Enjoy it."

The whirlwind surrounding me became an integral part of my body. The infinite mind of Creation filled me completely. I could see that It was the power that kept the whirlwind running.

Surges of infinite energy raced up and down my being. Increasing levels of that energy continued to flow into my being, lifting vibrational levels still higher. The golden radiance of the Eternal Presence intensified. Attunement to the Infinite Mind and Spirit continued. An eternity passed while total contact continued.

The rapture continued ever onward. Eternity had no beginning, no ending. It continued forever. All concept of time became meaningless. The Eternal Presence filled me with more radiant love. I wanted it to continue forever. Total acceptance into that level brought me the gift of everlasting life, yet I knew I must return, but when.

A faint glimmer of awakening brought with it returning awareness of the nearness of my two teachers, seated beside me in our favorite chairs. Yet the total contact with Creation remained. Although I knew reality would soon return, I wanted this contact to remain forever.

Remembrance of a childhood game called, "Who's got the power," emerged in my mind. Bedlam erupted with each child screaming loudly that he or she had that power, hoping to shout down those with weaker will power. Knowing that only God was omnipotent, I refused to participate.

My teachers understood. As their merged mind touched mine, they said, "Do not equate that memory with what you just had the privilege to experience."

"Nothing on earth could ever compare," I said. I am sorry if the extent of my contact gave you concern. When every aspect of Creation stood clearly revealed before me, my own responsibility not to interfere became equally clear. Could I really have caused harm?"

"Our concern for your success is so great, we didn't want a single thought to cross your mind that, however innocent it might have been, could alter the composition of the universe."

## Chapter XVIII

I said, "I have seen Tschen Li, you and others create the material things you need with a single thought. You have promised that some day I will be permitted to do the same. I shudder to think of what might have happened if at that moment, an idle thought of concern for earth had crossed my mind."

"And we cannot help or interfere unless someone asks," they said.

"You went all of the way," they continued. "something that rarely happens. Remember that you had eight angels helping you. They were all part of your spiritual family. Each one of them dedicated to helping you come back to Creation as soon possible. That should tell you how much we want you back."

"Thank you," I said. "When I bring some of my good students to this level for instruction, maybe we should not push too hard."

"Not to worry," they said. "Remember, you have been under our instruction for almost all of your lifetime. and that constitutes only one lifetime. Think of the many other times."

I will remember the above incident for a long time. They wanted it recorded here to let every student of the Masters' Meditation know that it is a philosophy, a way of life, and the ultimate road to ascension.

Like my own spiritual family that pushed me to the highest level, every person that practices this meditation with me will receive my assistance, and that of my guides as well as their own.

This meditation is not included among the original nine which constitute the mail order program. The last four tapes of that program deal with intense experiences in the angelic realm. By the time you complete that part of the course, you will be ready for a lifetime of pleasures such as this meditation.

At that time, you will be ready to explore the entire universe under the guidance of your own masters and teachers. Filled with the great love of the Creator, the Eternal Presence wraps you in its arms and protects you wherever you go.

In the presence of all of that, a successful life should be assured.

## Chapter XIX

### The Final Results

This was originally intended to be the ending chapter, bringing the masters' and angels' labor to a very satisfactory conclusion, and followed by the printed mediation. After all was finished, they added another exciting chapter, No. 20. You will find it well worth the effort.

My typing ability highlighted my own contribution to what became their monumental project to bring this information to as many inhabitants of the planet earth as possible. That, and my understanding of their own world developed over seventy-seven years of personal contact, enabled me to interpret their messages, and record them for the benefit of those who are concerned for their own future and that of our planet and the life that it supports.

Until now, the masters relied upon word of mouth advertising to spread notice of the existence of their own meditation and its many special benefits. The modest success of my first book, *Cosmic Fire*, brought additional meditators into our group.

As an unknown author writing about a little known and perhaps misunderstood subject, I lacked knowledge and the ability to advertise my work. My experiences over the past year and a half have changed that dramatically.

My own masters and angels have put me on a roller coaster ride of experiences over the entire length and breadth of the cosmos. The knowledge gained from these travels could change the lives and fortunes of every person on earth for the better. It is important to all of us to have that information brought to the attention of everyone, for the future of the planet itself is at stake.

It began during a few weeks preceding, and continued

onward from the near death journey they allowed me to make, that prepared me to view eternity in a more realistic manner than that permitted in the dream-like state of the meditation. We reported the clarity of that experience early in this book.

Mother Mary, an old friend of our group, came to us recently and offered to assist. With her came the archangel Raphael and a group of angels that worked with him and her. The changes brought by that help should excite our imagination with the promise it brings.

The increased energy accompanying their presence has already brought positive results. New people call us daily, and join with our meditative effort when they learn what we have and what we are trying to accomplish.

The statement of a new meditator who joined us yesterday tells us what is happening. She said, "When I heard that someone like you existed, I knew I had to meet you, to hear the message you bring to the world, to study with you and learn what you teach."

The power of the angelic message reaches out from that high level, and touches the heart of the many, who have previously sought in vain for answers to the mysteries of the universe and the life it supports.

For we must learn that the angelic realm is not only a dream, but a challenge. It has always been our birthright. It requires only half the effort to reclaim that birthright than to bear the rigors of existence demanded of those who choose to remain earthbound. The rewards from attaining that higher level are many thousand times greater than anything life on earth could possibly offer.

The weekly meetings of Mother Mary and Magnolia continue under my guidance. The energy increases, the

## Chapter XIX

messages become clearer and to the point. While each of these meetings are of great importance, until now, the last meeting proved to be the most productive.

In it, Mother Mary showed us how to use a healing method we have already learned, to share our energy and our concern with our beloved mother earth, who needs it so desperately now. We accomplished this through use of the Cosmic Whirlwind meditation which we covered earlier in this book.

In this session, we used the meditation to generate large quantities of Life Force energy, and while receiving within ourselves all of this energy we could use, with no restrictive limitation, we shared that energy with every other living thing on earth.

Then we used the whirlwind to take us into the angelic realm, and to the planet New Home and our favorite meeting place with the masters and angels. While following her usual guidelines, Mother Mary appears, mentally greets the other angels, and directs her attention to my guest, Magnolia and to me.

With their permission, I present part of the session dealing with Mother Mary's concern over the destructive use the people of earth make of earth's natural resources. In this, the greedy, negative mind set of the majority of earth's citizens plays an important part.

She has chosen this meditation and this book, to awaken the caring citizens of the planet to the danger, and to show each of them they can make a difference by using the remedies provided by the Masters' Meditation.

She appeared to us in the special meeting room. What follows is that part of the session in which she showed us graphically and in reality how each of our meditators could help in the healing of our beloved planet.

RALPH: "I ask you now to link your mind to the mind of Mother Mary, and to feel her great love descending upon you now. And I yield to you now, as your mind makes contact with that of Mother Mary."

MAGNOLIA: "The volume is so incredible My heart chakra is growing to a point where it is almost painful in a sweet kind of way. I feel such a powerful connection of this love energy. I feel it coming into me from the tree of life, from every chakra and from the cosmic whirlwind.

"I feel it going out through my hands. My hands are tingling as this energy is funneling through me like a flood. It's not a negative thing. It's like my channels are clear for the first time in a long time.

"And so it's this unbounded energy, love energy that's flowing through . And I can sense it going down into the earth You know how, when we do Reiki, sometimes it can be incredibly intense because the flow is so powerful. When there's a great need for this energy, you can sense it, and if you can open yourself completely and allow it to flow through. It's a phenomenal sensation.

"And I feel the earth just soaking it up. I feel Her transferring it through me, through us, as if we were a conduit for this love energy. I feel it going on down in and actually charging the batteries of the crystal network, so that it will store it so that the earth can use it. This is another aspect of what we can do in meditation.

"I am receiving multiple images of a kind of symbolic analogy where the earth is in kind of a hypothermic state for love energy. It's very difficult for the earth to generate its own love energy, it's own connection to the Eternal Presence.

## Chapter XIX

"And it is critical that we provide this, just as in human life, hypothermia is a life-threatening condition that requires a gentle warming. In critical conditions in the wilderness, they recommend that you actually get skin to skin with the hypothermic victim.

"And you allow their body to recharge through a gentle warming, slow warming. If it's done through medical knowledge, it's done in tepid baths. That slowly helps the body to regenerate its energy.

"And what is happening right now is that we are assisting the earth to recharge its Eternal Essence repository. Charging its battery, if you will. And it needs this, not just today but on a regular basis. I can see that this is going to be an aspect of future meditations on our own, and recommending to others who are also concerned about the state of health of the earth.

"We can channel, we can be conduits for this love energy. It's kind of, like we can be extension cords where we plug into the Eternal Presence, and we are allowing that energy to flow through us. And we are plugging into the earth, into the spiritual consciousness and into the earth's vibrations, and bathing the earth with this life and love energy that comes to us from God.

"And I can see Mary's face. She is beaming with joy. She feels the connection. She feels what is happening. She feels the earth absorbing, taking into itself this essential energy, this love energy.

"This ia a part of what we are to do. This is her sole purpose in her existence, to assist us to tap into the love energy, into the Eternal Presence of God that she embodies. And that's why we are associated with mothering, and motherhood and nurturing. She volunteered in the spiritual realm, to be the embodiment of this kind of unconditional motherly love

"I'm seeing flashes of our past two meditations where She was describing for us the process, and how important it is for us to be in tune with all of the many facets of the process.

"The end goal is to be clear lines, conduits, clear channels, in the sense of kind of a tube, a network. And through Reiki in particular we are opened already, and a tube already, to allow this energy to generate within our bodies and flow out through our hands. And it is just continuing. The absorption rate is so profound.

"She is showing me a kind of physical, geophysical manifestation of how this love energy can work. It's almost as if I see places on the earth where there are wounds, scars, located on the planet surface and below the surface.

"Its almost like witnessing a physical wound on a human that is rapidly healing beyond imagination, beyond belief. Where this open wound that is oozing pus and bacteria is being cleansed, and is actually healing up on a microbal level, on an anatomic level to the point where the scars are invisible. And it's beginning to heal to the point where nutrients are being remanifested through creative essence, the eternal essence, the creative processes.

"It's manifesting nutrients that are bringing back life into the once dead, lifeless rock, minerals. It's recharging the minerals It's actually manifesting plant life now, and I see moisture being collected in these places that were wasteland.

"I'm seeing the miraculous possibilities where. . . (in tears) Oh! It's so beautiful!

## Chapter XIX

"Excuse me, I was so overwhelmed for a moment."
RALPH: "That's all right."
MAGNOLIA: "It is, in fact, possible then. And the process has begun.

"I feel that She is gently reducing the amount of energy. Our attunement level will dictate how much energy we can channel for the earth, and for ourselves, of course. It certainly will affect our own attunement. The more energy that flows through, the higher our vibrational abilities will become."

The above consist of a twelve minutes vertibatim account of a twenty-four minute session where the mind of the meditator, Magnolia, was intimately attuned to the mind of Mother Mary.

Through this meditation, for many years I enjoyed many personal contacts in the angelic realm with this Great Lady, as well as many other famous and not so famous personalities from the past and in the present. Over that time, I deliberately chose not to divulge those frequent contacts. For obvious reasons, I broke with that custom at Mother Mary's request.

Her concern for the adverse condition now prevailing on earth led her to break her own silence in order to help us alert the citizens of her beloved planet earth to the dangers they are facing.

We discussed beforehand the alternate ways she could show Her concerns to earth's inhabitants. She wanted me to be the bearer of her message, but the reader would have only my unsupported word. Magnolia had worked with me for many years and was well versed in this already established meditative procedure.

Furthermore, we would have someone else to attest to the actuality of this contact and to the unbelievable results we could achieve. Furthermore, if it becomes necessary, with practice I can take almost any other fairly good meditator into the same process and achieve the same results, provided they are willing to sincerely cooperate.

In fact, the same is true with almost all of the facts I have reported in this book. With the right person and at the right time, I can demonstrate the efficacy of this powerful meditation, and the results that can be attained through its proper use

It is this confirmability that sets this meditation and its powerful results apart from all of the other attempted imitations.

The seeker of truth who reads this book is asked to remember these facts in beginning this study. It is like an unexpected delicacy that one rarely encounters. It excites the taste buds, and promises to endure the tests of time.

You can sample it with gusto, until you find that the rapture in each of its many avenues of delight increases with each return visit.

Perseverence is the key element to success. Contact with the inner self grows stronger with each meditation. A Study of the tenets of various self-help and self-healing groups that abound in our society, reveals that one's belief in the power of the inner self is the parallel word most often used by each of them.

Go within, bring your own life into balance, and you will find in the inner self, an opening of consciousness that embraces the mighty cosmos. It should be clear that the Masters' Meditation brings with it all of the necessary methods to help you achieve that goal.

## Chapter XX

### Mother Mary speaks.

At the conclusion of the last chapter, my master and teachers brought their message to an end. They had produced more than a year of information, which for me could well have encompassed an entire lifetime. All that remained would be a final review and publication.

But life otherwise continued at the same pace. In teaching the daily meditations and the many other duties that occupied my time, spectacular events continued at an even greater pace than before.

True to their promise, the additional masters and angels that joined our group from the angelic realm, helped us spread our message. They added their influence to the greater effort of those already working with us. We now had a much larger group of helpers, touching the minds of as many people on earth as they could, spreading the news in their own way. Their influence combined easily with ours and the results became evident in an increase in the number of people seeking our meditation. But we still have a long way to go.

Mother Mary had taken a special notice of me during the long years of my study of this meditation. She often came with Mataji and Mirva and let her presence add to the intensity of my spiritual contact.

Years of such intimate contact with the masters and angels, allowed me to become so accustomed to their presence, I found myself accepting it as a normal way of life. The almost instant availability of their assistance came to me whenever I asked.

My early conditioning led me to believe that my life on earth had no special meaning. Nothing in my life or presence on earth differed from that of the others around me. If these so-called miracles happened in my own life, surely everyone else enjoyed the same privilege. Much later I learned that while my early concepts were true, nothing could have been further from the truth in the actuality of the world around us.

When I began teaching, Mother Mary again favored us with occasional visits during my classes. Our students profited by the special energy from her presence, but not wishing to capitalize on her occasional visits, I had said very little of her continuing interest.

She surprised me with her increasing concern for our world. Now she often joined with Mataji and Mirva, and in their discussions with me during my special angelic realm meditative visits, she voiced her concern over the deteriorating conditions now so dangerously prevalent on planet earth.

My increasing awareness and growing consciousness enabled me to sense an overall guarded concern for our planet among the other angels and masters that came to be with us during those visits. It came to me in subtle tinges of thought riding on the wings of other messages they gave me.

None of them seemed inclined to tell me the specific nature of their concern. When I asked them directly, their usual comment was something like, "Even the angels in heaven are not aware of the date or the time or the nature of any occurrence that was destined to occur." But behind all of that lay a pictorial impression of everyone on earth dropping into an enormous bottomless pit.

The fact that other so-called new age prognosticators flooded the world with graphic predictions of doom and

## Chapter XX

certain destruction, did nothing to help the situation. They had nothing to offer other than their dire predictions, with little more information other than their prophesies.

On the other hand, our masters and angels advised us only of the possibility of incompatible changes that would occur on earth. Theirs was a message of hope, it need not occur if enough people found and began to practice the masters' and angels' own meditation.

This solution offered each person an opportunity to improve the value of his or her own life. At the same time, their newly-found positive attitudes would join with that of many others on this path. When they reached the meditative level where contact with the secret power of the universe occurred, that mind-influenced positive attitude would increase exponentially.

That effect is comparable to the explosion of tiny atoms. Each atom exploding others until within a microsecond the power of an atomic bomb is released.

Contact with the secret power of the universe produces the same increase of energy but with opposite results. That energy is the life and love of God for humanity. It flows within the meditator first. There the multiplication factor enables it to fill his or her body, where his or her life-enhancing healing power attends their own needs first. Then it spreads outward to the benefit of mother earth and every living thing thereon.

The masters and angels continue to assist in any way they can. They will stand by us all of the way, but the final result is our own responsibility. It is up to us. If enough of us cannot leave off our greed and self indulgent behavior and turn our thoughts to our own salvation, then we alone will bear the blame for our shortsightedness.

Those of us who try to help, and take our stand with the masters and angels, will as the result of the Masters' Meditation, find their way across the bridge leading to what the angels call eternity. It is a no lose situation, and it is as simple as that.

In an earlier chapter I told how Mataji and Mirva gave me a graphic presentation of the angels' view of the deplorable conditions existing on earth at this time. Their composite view seemed surprisingly accurate. It made me ashamed of the tragic disposition shown by the great number of my fellow human beings, and of their inhuman treatment of their own kind.

Compared with the five or more billion persons living on our planet at is time, those who have learned the masters' meditation might be small in number. But the multiplication factor attending the positive energy we are able to produce is already beginning to make a difference. As more meditators are drawn to our side, the energy they produce will join with that of ours.

The energy of the angels will join that of our own. We have within our grasp the possibility of breaking the grip that evil has upon our future. It is up to us to bring enough additional workers to our side to make the difference. Our teachers believe that we can eventually accomplish that goal. The future existence of planet earth depends upon it.

Mother Mary asked that this extra chapter be added to the book. She felt that this additional knowledge that came to us a little later should be made public, and that it would help clarify much of that which had been given before.

She has intensified her efforts to bring her ideas and

## Chapter XX 167

feelings to the attention of our world that she loves completely. She wishes to help us accomplish our goal by letting everyone who will listen know of her concern and continued desire to help in any way she can.

Some of our members report they have sensed her presence during meditation. Others report a special blessing from the vision of a beautiful angel attending their session. They felt it could only have come from her.

Others ask me to take them into her presence during the meditation that I teach. I make room during those special meditations for "an important person" to contact those individuals. In some cases another important person makes contact. In others, Mother Mary will come with a special greeting and blessing.

These meditations are becoming more powerful, with enduring benefits that follow the students into their daily lives. The increased spiritual vibrations attending each meditative session raises everyone's consciousness to ever higher levels. Contact with Creation's eternal presence fills them with rapture and sensations of lasting peace. None of earth's transient pleasures could even remotely compare with the joy that fills their daily lives.

Some of the more advanced students, who have learned to meditate on their own, have reached the level where they can contact other special persons at the height of this meditation. Contact at this level is rewarding.

In an incident of special interest to us at this time is a young woman who asks to be called Maria. She has been meditating with me for many years. She has become an excellent meditator, and has advanced to an extremely high level of awareness.

I always seek an audience before asking Mother Mary

to make an appearance. At other times, she will come to us of her own volition. When I took Maria into her usual private meditation, much to her surprise Mother Mary made one of her unexpected visits. The glorious vision of her angelic appearance, and the surrounding flow of her spiritual energy and love overwhelmed the young woman. It left her literally speechless.

The masters allowed me the privilege to witness, and even to participate in the spiritual contact. In my work with them, I had grown accustomed to the presence of angels. Maria had gradually accepted her masters. She now accepted their advice and guidance without question, not even suspecting they were also angels. When Mother Mary appeared, Maria automatically knew who it was. Not only that, she knew she was in the presence of what to her was the most holy of all angels. Never in her life had she ever suspected she would have such a divine privilege.

Mataji and Mirva had assisted me in bringing Maria to my private box in this theater-like assembly room on the planet New Home. In spirit, we were allowed to visit the angelic realm under the guidance of the masters.

Maria was seated at my right side, with two of our masters seated in front us. Unseen to Maria, a host of angels had accompanied the Holy Mother as she came to be with us. Many of the angels took seats beside and behind us. Others floated gracefully in a large area above.

Deep in meditation, Maria felt the powerful presence of the Holy Mother as she descended into the chair in front of her. I sensed her great mind as it reached out and embraced that of the woman at my side. Overcome with emotion and love, Maria could not respond in so much as

## Chapter XX

a thought. Tears filled her eyes, and she wept in silence, sobbing uncontrollably.

From the minds of my masters and that of Mother Mary, came a picture that told the whole story. The simple faith of Maria and the love she had always felt for the mother of Jesus, had attracted the angels' attention. Maria's love for the masters' and angels' meditation had led her into extremely high levels of spiritual development. Her dedication and purity of thought led them to select her as a special messenger to bring the news of Mother Mary's concern to the world. In her wisdom, the Holy Mother would make contact and prepare Maria for what they wanted her to do.

Mother Mary allowed the radiant light of her magnetic presence to surround the weeping Maria. I could feel the splatter of genuine tears flowing freely and falling upon her face, arms and hands. My mind joined that of the special angel seated before us, as it cradled Maria in its arms, and expanded outward to include me in its embrace.

Soothing sensations of love and belonging continued to surround and embrace Maria. As time passed slowly, instructions for me alone flowed to me along the same line of communication.

Mother Mary said, "Please remain here with her as long as you can. She has been conditioned by her faith to consider contact with me an impossibility. Her tears flow from joy and love, and I will remain in contact long enough to accustom her to my presence. Then you can take her back.

"Work with her as much as you can. Bring her back here as often as possible. I will come again to her each time she comes. It will require a few more sessions like this before she can accept my presence without excessive emotion. We need her as our special messenger.

"As before, continue with the others as you have in the past. Maria's simple love is the purest form of contact we have with your world. She will help us in places where no one else can.

"I haven't told you this before, but all of us treasure your lifetime of devotion. Yours is the rarest kind of love, it is unconditional. Maria has the same love. For that reason we have chosen her to help."

In the silence that followed, I watch the sobbing subside into gentle sighs. Sensations of heavenly love intensified. We entered into the rapture of the moment, following the ecstasy of the contact to unimaginable levels of exultation.

Time stood still. It could have been hours, days or even weeks, we knew not which. The aspect of time ceased to exist. We were at home, with God, with the angels. In complete harmony with Creation, we drifted on and on in timeless immersion in a limitless ocean of an eternity of God's presence and love.

I knew not whether we slept or drifted timelessly in a dimension of unknowingness. Hours had passed before the first glimmer of returning consciousness nudged gently into my enraptured mind. More asleep than awake, I dozed fitfully, clinging happily to an ocean of unconditional love and the mantle of the Eternal Presence that embraced me.

In a soft recliner to my right, the sleeping Maria lay quietly. The happy smile on her face told me more than words could ever tell. She was at peace, resting quietly, and reliving every precious moment of her first contact

## Chapter XX

with the Holy Mother.

I tiptoed softly out of the room and returned to my study, and activated my computer. Every atom within me retained the vibrations from our high level contact. Every memory of that beautiful contact remained indelibly fixed in my entranced mind. As my fingers touched the keyboard, they effortlessly began writing the words you are now reading.

Mother Mary had instructed me to write my version of this contact, to alert every reader of this book to the unique possibilities found in this, the masters' and angels' meditation. She wants you to know that to those who study and master this special meditative method, contact with the angelic realm and those who reside in that dimension is possible. Anyone can do it. Once you know it exists, the only barrier resides in your own mind.

Maria's first contact with Mother Mary was reported in detail. The angels wanted you to know, to see and feel the love, rapture and beauty that awaits those who seek and find the way. Words cannot even begin to describe any one aspect of the contact, let alone the entire event. If you can see and feel even a small part of my experience, use your imagination and visualize it as much greater, more beautiful and impressive.

If you become a student of the meditation, enjoy the wonderful benefits accompanying each level along the way. Know in your heart that many angels await you as you increase in ability with each higher level you are able to attain. It's a promise they always keep.

Mother Mary told Maria that anyone could attain that level if they really wanted to Maria was anxious to repeat the meditation. She worked gamely through three more meditations, each one becoming less emotional, but the tears continued to come at the height of the contact.

I wish she would allow me to duplicate the tapes for the public to hear the tremendous impact the presence of the Holy Mother makes upon those she contacts. You could share her emotions and feel the magic of the Holy Mother's presence.

The advanced students of this meditation can make the same contact with many important beings out of our past. By that time they have become accustomed to working with angels. The pure love that flows between Maria and Mother Mary is special. She has permitted me to allow you to read her part of her fifth contact.

This part begins after I have gone through a long procedure bringing her to the angelic realm, and allowing her to be seated with me among the angels in my special area of contact on the planet New Home.

MARIA: "I was just telling Mother Mary that sometimes I don't feel worthy of the privilege, I am just a simple girl. And she's telling me that everyone is worthy. Everyone who wants to come here, who wants to be in my presence, who wants to help me, who asks for my help, everyone is worthy.

"Our problem on our planet is, we do not love ourselves enough. And because of that, our self-worth is small. But if we would love ourselves, we would know how much she loves us. And just the fact that we ask, that's all that's needed. Just ask if you want to come, but you have to ask

"I feel so good in her presence. It's such peace, such tranquillity. I know that there is no place on earth that feels as good as when I am here in her presence. This is

## Chapter XX 173

just, you cannot describe the feeling.

"She is so happy that I have come back again. She said that one must be very faithful, and that's what wrong with most of the others. They are not faithful. This is not just for one time or two times. This is forever. But, we have free will, and if we don't want to come back. We don't have to.

"This is why she's telling me again how important faith is.. First of all, in ourselves, in what we can achieve we must have strong overpowering faith. And then the faith in them, and the faith of what we can do together. They will come half way if we come half way. Only then can we learn. Only then can we go to higher levels.

"She's talking about vibrations again. They will become so refined, so sensitive that we will know immediately of anything that is wrong around us. And we will know how to deal with it and how to protect ourselves, because the sensitivity is coming from them. It's like a frequency, and if we are on this very high frequency the sensitivity is right behind it. And we will learn how to tune in.

She is also telling me that this is not for everyone. Not every soul is developed on the same level. Every soul is where it needs to be. I guess this is where the expression old souls and new souls comes from, because of what the soul has learned. It's not what the body has learned. It's not important what the body is learning, it's what the soul and the mind are learning.

"And this is why we must accept all soul levels. We must have understanding. And most of all we must help the souls that want to come up to a higher level, and are struggling so hard and just need this extra help. And when our soul knows without doubt that there is another soul a little bit lower that it can help in a very gentle way, this is very important because this is where your higher levels will be. Only then can we develop, grow, and evolve to a level we never dreamed of.

"We all have the same potential. Everybody has the same gift. Only some cannot see it because they are not developed. Others don't want to see it because their vibrations are so low they can't feel anything. In order to feel this, you have to listen within yourself. Not the noise without, but this very refined feeling within.

"Mother Mary is telling me that she is happy that we have already involved so many of our friends with the healing of our planet, with the healing of our frequencies around us, our vibrations. They seem to be not as dull any more, as dark and as low, that's the only way I can say it. It is off key. We are starting to be attuned, like a violin or a piano. We are attuning our vibrations to the healing of the whirlwind, of the meditation, of the tree of life. Whatever we can think of, it makes no difference.

"The thought form is so important. We have to keep this positive thought form, very high, very lovely, very beautiful thought forms. This is how we create very wonderful vibrations about us.

"Oh, Mother Mary, I hope I am saying all of this right. Okay! Thank you! I never knew this was so simple. I thought there was a lot more to it, a lot more work involved. But it's so simple. We humans are complicated, yes. But unless we complicate everything, we are not happy. It is our own inadequacy. We need to learn to become more sure of ourselves. First you must learn to have faith in yourself, only then you can have faith in us.

## Chapter XX

"Mother Mary is telling me that she is with us at every meditation that's done in your home. And she said that she is looking down upon us with such love. She's so thankful about what we are doing. And she said that we should visualize that she is looking down at us with such pleasure. She's so happy that we are doing our part, and she wants me to tell everybody how grateful she is. Even though we are only doing so very little, she is telling me that is all that is needed to make the difference

"Some problems within our planet can not be changed, especially our waters, the oceans. All the animals in the oceans, in the waters, they are all crying because of what we are doing with all the poisons. And this has to be cleaned up. We have to clean up all of this poison. And in order for this poison to leave all of our oceans, something major will have to happen.

"But the earth itself, the planet that we live on, and. all the underground. All the devastation, the ground, etc. can be helped in many ways through our healing. She can hear the crying, the pain from our trees, the waters, fields, everything is dying because of the poisons.

"We should have started this at least ten years ago. But she is telling me that it is never too late. And what we have done here in your home with our friends that help and meditate with us, has already made a big difference. She is helping all of us, and we have to thank you (Mary) for helping us. You are the one that did it. And she tells me, my child, we are *all* in this together. This is why we have to all work together. And it's not just you, or me or anybody else. Together, that's how we can make a difference. Together.

"She is telling me that we will all know the right kind

of people, the right kind of souls that we can touch. That we will know the right ones to help us. We will know. She's making a special effort to have these souls come to us, to reach out for us in many different ways. And we will know. And more and more will be coming. This will be her part. This will be her help. She will send all of these people that need our help and in turn will help us.

"And I am happy to be with you. I love you too ,I love you so very much. Everyone I know loves you too. And you can feel it, yes, I know. We are all special, yes.

"She is also telling me that all we have to do is give one thought and she will be here. And she will guide us. And she will make every effort. She will never ever turn anybody down, but we need to ask for her help. She can not come to us unless we ask. And this is our big problem. Most people don't know, or even want to know.

"But we will help. We will do all we can. Life can become beautiful again. It can become a paradise as it was in the beginning. And for that I thank you. All of my friends thank you. I know you are telling me that thank you is not necessary. But I don't know how else to express myself. Yes, you are telling me that you already know. I don't have to speak the words. Yes.

"It's so beautiful here. There are so many of them here, I think I know them, but I guess it's not important. I just know they are here, and I feel their love."

Maria closes, seeing the presence of the host of angels around us, and feeling their love.

As usual in my meditations, Mataji and Mirva helped us make the spiritual transition from the earthly plane to the highest level of the angelic.

## Chapter XX

Maria mentioned how easily she contacted Mother Mary. She spoke from the high level we had already attained where many miracles are possible for those who have attained this height.

For eons of time, Mataji has been custodian of this special method of Creative contact with what they call the Masters' and Angels' Meditation. I had told Maria of the angels Mary and Raphael bringing their influence to our group, and when Mary appeared to Maria, Maria already knew of that promise to help and the purpose of their help. That is why the specific help was not mentioned in this account of the contact.

Of importance here is the continuing contact Maria has with Mother Mary. Information is now coming to her in such a great quantity that Maria might very well become the spokesperson for Mother Mary here on earth. Once the meditation is mastered, such contact and the information therefrom is easily attained.

The reader may have already become aware of the ever-increasing intensity of personal contact between me and my spiritual teachers following the near death episode reported in Chapter IV and Chapter V of this book. In the almost two years and literally hundreds of personal visits to the angelic realm that have occurred since that time, my awareness of the totality of the massive cosmos as part of that realm has been expanded to infinite levels.

My personal meditations with the advanced students that study with me have also reached more powerful levels. Some have advanced to heights that enable them to make preliminary visits to the angelic realm under my guidance and that of our teachers.

Consider the powerful benefits obtainable by sincere

students of this meditation. Spiritual visits to the wonders of the angelic realm are easily attainable. These seekers of wisdom no longer have to take the unsupported word of someone else. They can learn to see and experience the entire scope of the cosmos for themselves. During these sessions, the wisdom of the universe is an open book, readily available for their spiritual awakening. With it come a wisdom seldom attained by the inhabitants of earth who seek only its limited pleasures.

And with that priceless knowledge comes the wisdom to happily complete their allotted time here on earth, while enjoying constant contact with the angelic realm at the same time.

In the beauty of such an existence, the duality of life becomes a reality. The meditator enjoys the best of both worlds, secure in the knowledge that eternal life awaits, either at the end of this incarnational experience or sooner if it becomes necessary.

As Mother Mary mentioned so many times, "Just do it." Every little effort, thought, or deed can make a great difference. And the angels will do their part by working with us. With only a few sincere souls working together from this level, the end results can become astounding. As others join with us and add their energy to our own, our force can expand to the point of first balancing the opposing forces, then nullifying and replacing the negative with the positive. With just a few sincere helpers, we can succeed.

What better way can there be to lay up treasures for yourself in heaven for an eternity, and not here on earth where our visit is only temporary.

## Chapter XXI

### THE MEDITATION

This is an actual process that I often use to lead a new student into meditation for the first time. By now, you should be familiar with the procedure. If you have no one to read the following process to you, read it into your tape recorder using a soothing, well modulated, voice. While the length of the meditation is about 30 minutes, choose a longer tape. This will eliminate the problem of timing your reading, enabling you to devote your full attention to the dictation.

When reading the meditation into a tape recorder, you should begin about five paragraphs below with the words, "Fix your mind completely on my voice." Speak slowly and positively, pronouncing each word clearly. When you have finished, rewind the tape to the beginning. You are now ready to begin.

With practice, you will find it easy to meditate anywhere and at any time. In the beginning, you should find a location that will insure complete privacy. Silence your phone, and ask other members of your household not to disturb you for the next hour.

Sit comfortably in a chair, your head erect, your feet flat on the floor, your hands in your lap, palms upward. You may sit in the lotus position if you wish. Close your eyes, consciously begin to relax your entire body and listen to the voice of the speaker.

The following is most important: Throughout the entire meditation, use your imagination fully and visualize within your mind every scene described to you by the voice of the speaker.

The six lines in quotation marks below should be

repeated three times each. You are now ready to begin.

    Begin reading here: ------>

Fix your mind completely on my voice. Pay particular attention to my voice. Make each word I say your own by repeating it silently to yourself. Throughout this entire meditation, use your imagination fully and vividly picture in your mind each scene that is described to you by my voice. Use your imagination now and relax each part of your body as I ask you to do so.

      "Your arms and legs are completely relaxed."
      "Your abdomen is warm and comfortable."
      "Your heartbeat is calm and regular."
      "Your breathing is calm and relaxed."
      "You are now completely relaxed."
      "Your mind is quiet and still."

Visualize a very large, misty golden aura completely surrounding your body. Out of that aura flows a wave of blissful relaxation, entering every part of your body at the same time. You can feel every nerve, muscle, cell and fiber of your entire body relaxing completely and perfectly, and you allow your consciousness to flow within and seek that center of everything that you are. That perfect center of your entire being now completely surrounds your consciousness. You are now perfectly centered and completely relaxed.

With your consciousness centered deep within, and your mind responsive to higher levels of perception, you allow your intuitive awareness to merge with that vortex of energy emanating from the earth below. You see and feel that energy moving upward from the center of the earth; swirling upward in a counter clockwise motion. The energy completely encircles your body as it moves in and flows into every nerve, muscle, cell and fiber of your entire being.

As the warming vibrations of energy flow upward into your body, you are also aware of a beam of golden light emanating from the highest center of energy above and spiraling earthward in a counter clockwise motion, completely encircling your body as it descends and merges with the light of the energy emanating from the earth below.

From the juncture of those energies, a magnificent golden aura completely encircles your being and protects you from all outside influence, except that of your guides, your masters, the ascended masters, the angels and the sound of my voice.

Within the center of that ray of golden light flows an animated beam of energy that falls softly upon the top of your head. You sense its vitalizing aliveness as sensations of golden energy surround your entire being. Even with your eyes closed, you are aware of the rays of brilliant sunlight that embrace you, flowing around your body from every direction and entering into your being through the top of your head. The beam of energy expands as it flows into your body at that location and continues flowing down your body like liquid sunshine, filling it to capacity from the top of your head to the tips of your toes. It fills every part of your entire being completely and perfectly.

And now, as you feel that energy flowing within you, it begins to fill each of your major energy centers and continues to flow until they are filled to capacity. As these centers fill with this powerful energy, they begin to grow larger and blossom out in rays of golden radiance, sending fingers of gold and white light outward into the heavens where they reach and merge with the universal presence, that eternal presence of Creation itself.

As those lights merge with the eternal presence, each of the corresponding energy centers within you are attuned to the highest level of energy within the universe. As that attunement takes place, you feel your entire body coming into perfect balance. And when that balance is complete, you feel every part of your body receiving energy and achieving a perfect balance from the healing energy of the universe accompanying the inflow of that energy within you.

Filled with that golden light and with the attunement from Creation itself, your physical body begins to feel very light. As you relax where you are, you feel yourself becoming so light that your body begins to move up into the air in perfect comfort and safety. Higher and higher it floats gently up into the air, borne on the wings of that magnificent beam of golden light.

In perfect comfort and safety you float ever onward and upward now. You feel those shining rays of golden light surrounding your body. Embraced now in the arms of the beams of light, you feel the high frequency beams of that light flowing into your body, and every muscle, nerve and cell of your body begin to feel the increasing vibrations as the density of the earth is left behind and the surrounding light continues to vibrate at ever higher levels, in harmony with the higher vibratory levels descending from above.

As you continue to float onward and upward into the sky, you see the moon and the sun fading into the distance, with the sun becoming smaller and dimmer as it

## Chapter XXI

recedes into the darkness behind you until it becomes a tiny pinpoint of light in the canopy of heaven.

As you float ever onward and upward now, you approach the highest levels of the ascendancy. You see now before you the magnificent portals of the beautiful temple of lights. There you see within those portals, the reflection of the white and golden light that flows from above, reflecting from the stately columns of the temple millions of tiny rainbows. A limitless quantity of rainbows reflected from the crystalline surface of the temple, caressing you all over with the multiplicity of colors. You can feel the vibrations within your body growing stronger as you continue to approach those stately portals. In front of you, you see a long, narrow corridor.

Filled with the gold and white light, it is a corridor of rainbows, reflected from the crystalline surface of the ceiling, walls and floor. As you continue to float through the corridor of rainbows, headed into the spacious temple, you come to rest on a beautiful, white chair that is located in the geometric center of the temple of lights.

As you come to rest, you find your body supine on that comfortable chair, every contour of your body supported perfectly. From above, through a portal in the center of the ceiling, a beam of white and golden light descends, falling gently upon your body with the warming rays of blended golden light flowing gently into the surface of your flesh. The golden light is moving into your body now, moving deeper and deeper within as these rays of light fill the interior of your body to capacity.

This is the universal life force energy, the essence of life itself, flowing within you now, and you feel the creative urge of life within you as your awareness moves ever onward and upward now. Your consciousness, your vibrations flowing faster and faster, matching the accelerating vibrations of the temple of lights which surrounds you. As the accelerating vibrations of the white light flow within you, and the tingling sensations within you grow stronger, every nerve, muscle, cell and fiber of your body is raised to higher and higher levels of vibrations.

Now, as all of this takes place, you are aware that an ascended master, Master Rupon, has taken a position standing behind you. As you look, you see his friendly face, with dark hair, dark eyes, wearing a small mustache and beard. Observe that he is wearing in the customary white robe of an ascended master.

He reaches out and places his hands on top of your head, his fingers upon your forehead, and you feel the downpouring of what he calls the cosmic fire filling the area under his hands, the area of your forehead which lies between your eyes, known as the third eye, filling it to capacity in a moment of time.

More and more of this cosmic fire flows into your third eye, and you can feel the pressure building within you now as this essence of every atom in the universe, gathered by the hands of Master Rupon, continues to flow into your forehead.

This essence is drawn from the atoms that are the motivating power, energizing the entire universe. Master Rupon has gathered this energy that is flowing into your third eye now. Although your third eye is already filled to capacity, the energy continues to flow and the residue begins to spread, moving outward into the rest of your body. It leaves a tingling sensation within you and in

## Chapter XXI

every muscle of your physical body.

This powerful energy fills every part of your body which is tingling, alive and aglow to the powerful force of the cosmic fire, the essence of all of the energy of the universe. It continues to flow into you from the hands of Master Rupon.

Within your third eye you begin to feel an expansion of consciousness and your awareness begins to expand as it roams throughout the entire universe. Your Spiritual powers are now being opened at this high level to higher and higher limits through the powerful hands of Master Rupon. And this energy will continue throughout this entire meditation.

Allow your consciousness now to become aware of the presence of another ascended master. See him standing on your left side by your shoulder. If you don't already know that master, see him dressed in a white robe, both hands on your shoulders with the powerful master's energy pouring from the hands and flowing throughout your body; attuning your energy to the energy of that master and to the universe.

I want you to look at the hair, its style and color; look at the color of the eyes, look at the face and note any special feature such as race or skin texture, and, most of all, the gender. Memorize that face, feel the touch of the mind of that master upon your mind. As you feel the touch of your master's mind upon your own, if you don't know the called name of your master, now is the time to ask. Simply form the words in your mind, "What is your name?" Ask it mentally and accept the first answer that comes to you. That will be the name of your own ascended master.

Now, standing on your right side is another ascended master, also dressed in a white robe, with hands on your shoulders and energy flowing into your body from those hands. As before, see the hair, the style and color, the color of the eyes, any special facial feature. As with your own ascended master, ask the gender because they can appear either as male or female. Look, observe, feel the touch of the mind of this master and as with the other, ask, "What is your name," and accept the first answer that comes into your mind.

This ascended master is your master/teacher. A person that will be with you and has been with you as a guardian angel for most of your life. Now that conscious contact has been made, this master will always be near, within hearing distance of your voice whenever you call. All you have to do is ask, and by coming into the temple of lights and putting yourself in this special chair, you have asked that your masters come to you.

As you lie there in your chair, I want you to look in the direction of your feet. You will see the figure of another ascended master standing at your feet. He is also dressed in a white robe, one that glistens and shines, brilliantly illuminated by the glowing golden aura which surrounds him completely from head to feet. He has deep blue eyes that shine like glowing sapphires, and an impressive face radiating outward beams of pure unconditional love.

He has brought to you the healing energy, and the intelligence of the creator, the energy that motivates the entire universe. He now walks slowly up your left side and takes a position behind you that is adjacent to that of Master Rupon. He reaches out and places his hands atop those of Master Rupon, and as they touch there is a dowmpouring of golden light that fills the interior of your head to capacity in an instant of time. That energy flows on down, filling your chest and your heart, your solar plexus, your lower abdomen, and on down your legs to your feet and ankles.

It fills your entire body in an instant of time, filling you to utmost capacity now, from that beautiful beam of golden light. Now that golden light is merging with the white light and the cosmic fire to form a more perfect light within you, a golden light which is representative of the eternal consciousness of the cosmic and it fills you to utmost capacity and is flowing strongly out of your body now through every pore of your skin. It forms a golden aura which surrounds you completely and perfectly. And that aura is continuing to grow as the light continues to flow into your body from the hands of the Master Healer.

Your body is filled to capacity. The golden aura now surrounding you reaches out beyond the temple of lights and beyond the mountain itself, reaching out beyond everything you have ever experienced as it flows into the universe. You feel like you are in the center of a golden sun with the surrounding aura flowing outward like brilliant sunshine.

You are now surrounded by the consciousness of the cosmic, that great awareness of all that there is. Feel the vibrations of the consciousness within your body growing stronger and stronger, lifting that consciousness to a higher level.

Some day in the future, as you continue to come to the temple of lights and fill yourself with this pulsating golden light which is the consciousness of the cosmic, you will find that your own vibrations will have increased with each visit and one day you will experience a harmonic vibration that will link your own awareness more closely with that of the great cosmic consciousness.

But for the moment, you are to enjoy the present harmonic blend you have attained with that cosmic awareness, because you are filled and surrounded with the sublime vibrations of the cosmic consciousness. You are now in complete contact with that supreme consciousness, you allow that golden light to cleanse and purify you, and find within it the promise that if you continue to come within the perimeter and allow it to fill your body, each time that you do your own consciousness will be lifted a little higher. That should be your purpose in life, the eternal contact with this great and beautiful cosmic consciousness.

And now, filled with that golden light and that great consciousness, surrounded by that aura flowing out of that golden light, the sensation of weightlessness returns and you find yourself floating gently out of the chair, drifting upward on the wings of the golden light that surrounds you. Feeling as free as a bird, you float up into the air. Your two masters are at your side and they are taking you higher and higher into the breath taking enchantment which surrounds you.

And still you allow your consciousness to rise, soaring higher and higher now you see in front of you a wide pathway, leading into a beautiful garden. You allow your body to descend and feel your feet touch the ground and you find yourself slowly strolling down the garden path under the guidance of your two masters, one of your masters walking on each side of you. All the while, you

## Chapter XXI

remain filled with the intense golden light, still in the center of that compelling cosmic consciousness that continues to envelop you.

You continue to walk slowly, filled with the breathtaking beauty of a myriad of flowers of all description along the border of each side. In front of you, in the center of the garden, you see a cleared section containing a semi-circular bench.

Your masters lead you to this location and allow you to sit in the center of that comfortable bench where you feel your body surrounded by high-frequency vibrations that reach into the center of your being and mingle with your own inner vibrations that struggle to reach their own high level, seeking always to attain a state of haramonium.

You now feel your vibrations merging nearer and nearer to those of the garden as they work to continue to lift your own ever higher in order to merge completely with those that now surround you.

You sense a tinge of coolness surrounding you and you feel that the sun has just disappeared below the distant horizon. A few of the brightest stars now appear dimly in the evening sky. It is a beautiful summer evening. Your two masters are sitting, one on each side of you and you feel your consciousness opening to communication with the consciousness of creation.

Your master that was sitting on your left side stands up and moves to a position in front of you. For the first time, you now see the full features of your own ascended master. He reaches out and places his hands on the top of your head. You experience the unusual feeling of the downpouring of the golden light of creation itself, flowing into your body.

Open your mind now to this master for the messages that will come to you will be simple but important. Thoughts, such as these, will come into your mind, "We will come to you whenever you ask. Here, in your own beautiful garden, you can enter into the silence as was the custom of others over the past centuries. Here you can allow that consciousness of the cosmic to flow within you. Here you can abide in the power and glory of the higher consciousness whenever you wish, as long as one of us are with you. Here you can speak with any master in the universe, all you have to do is ask. As you sit here in deep meditation, any information that you want can be yours.

"All you need to do is continue to come into the temple of lights and allow that to become one of the main purposes of your life. Then you can come into this garden, sit and meditate amid its many wonders, feel the mighty energy of the universe surrounding you and communicate with the Akashic records, with angels, with patriarchs of the past, kings, emperors, anyone you wish who is on this side of creation. All of this will be brought to you when you are ready if you but request it."

These and other messages are representative of those your masters will give you at first but this is only the beginning. Personal contact with your masters will improve with each meditation, limited only by your ability and your imagination. Use that imagination fully each time your masters bring you to the temple of lights. You have been shown the way; you now have control of your own future.

Your master now moves to your side and, with the assistance of the master on your right, they help you to

## Chapter XXI 191

your feet. The time has come for you to return to the temple. One on each side, they take you by the hand and you now feel yourself walking slowly out of the garden. You are reluctant to leave the harmony of your garden but you can return with your masters whenever you ask.

You are now floating gently back to the temple of lights where you find yourself still lying in the white chair, surrounded by your masters, still filled with the glowing rays of the golden light that is the consciousness of the cosmic.

Now, the hands of your own masters lift you gently out of the chair. You take one last look around you as you stand in front of the chair, and mentally thank everyone present for allowing you the privilege of visiting the temple, the schoolhouse of the masters.

You now see yourself walking slowly out of the temple, descending back to earth on that magnificent beam of golden light, aware that your own masters are still with you.

To expedite your return, I am now going to count from one to three. When I complete the count of from one to three you will find yourself in the room that you left, still in a deep state of relaxation. One...two...three. You are back in this room now, still in a deep state of relaxation.

I will awaken you in a moment but, before I do I want to remind you that you can and will remember everything that transpired, and you will take back into your own world the memory of everything that happened as well as all of the powerful healing energy and peace you now feel.

Now, at the count of from one to five you will awake, feeling good, happy to be alive. Number one, life is returning to your arms and your legs. Number two, coming up easy now. Number three, life is returning to the rest of your body. Number four, you are almost awake. Number five, you can open your eyes, now, and awake. You are feeling good, full of energy, and very, very happy.

---oooOooo---

This completes an actual processes, similar to those that I use in teaching meditation. I explained earlier that a single tape, containing the same identical words, should not be used over a prolonged period of time. This would cause the tape to lose its effectiveness since your subconscious mind quickly memorizes its contents causing you to become bored by the repetitions.

The problem does not exist in my classes. While I always follow the same order of presentation, I speak extemporaneously and the sequence of words are never the same. When students cannot attend my classes, I furnish them with four meditations, (two sides of two tapes). The meditations are similar, the connecting words are always different. This brings us closer to the viable process that I use in my classes.

These tapes are available by contacting the publisher of this book. They are inexpensive. You can write for information, or simply send $25, P&H included, with your request for the first set of tapes. Full instructions for their use will be included.

I close, wishing each of you success both in your studies and in your many future meditations.

**THE END**